Pho Families

A Parents' Guide to Life in the Valley of the Sun

Michelle Burgess

Illustrated by

Hillary and Haley Kay Burgess

ISBN 0-929526-43-0

Hot To Go Publishing
A Subsidiary of Phoenix Publishing Group
4123 North Longview
Phoenix, Arizona 85014
(602) 996-7129
www.phoenixpublishinggroup.com

I would like to thank my husband, Mike, and my children, Hillary, Haley Kay and Jack, for their patience and support throughout this undertaking. Thanks, too, to my girls for letting me use their beautiful artwork!

Also, I want to express my appreciation to the Powers That Be at Raising Arizona Kids magazine for giving me a professional home of which I can be proud, and for having the flexibility to encourage me in this project.

This book is dedicated to my mother, Suzanne Owens. Her love and support have been unconditional throughout my life, and it is a privilege and an honor to have learned from her how to live my life as a mother and as a person. She will never know how much she is appreciated.

How this book came to be

The first four and a half years I lived in the Valley, I kept pretty much to a 5-square-mile area. This was college, so what did I need beyond the University, a handful of movie theaters and an all-night Denny's or two?

Then I moved away, had three kids and began to see things in a whole new light. My priorities shifted; after all, what good is an all-night Denny's to someone who never goes out after dark?

When after seven years my family and I returned to the Valley, I came back to a sort of parallel universe. Not only had the area grown quite a bit, but it now had parks! And a zoo! And T-Ball and hiking and dairy farms and family-night ticket packages to hockey games and story times at the library! Was it possible that they had always been here, right under my nose, without my ever having noticed? Probably so, but I hadn't needed them the first time around.

So I set about rediscovering the Phoenix area, and in the process grew excited at the seemingly endless list of all there is to see and do here. I came to realize how lucky we are to live in the Valley, with its unique combination of big-city amenities and off-the-beaten-path treasures.

In writing this book I have attempted to construct a sort of timeless, user-friendly guide/directory hybrid. More than 95 percent of the sites and attractions listed are within an hour's drive of anywhere in the Valley, although a few annual festivals are a bit farther away. Much of it is arranged by region, and I've tried to list cross streets whenever possible.

If your family is new here, I wish you luck in getting to know your magnificent new home. But even if you've lived here all your life, I'm sure that you have discovered the same thing I did: When you have kids, it's a whole new world out there.

Enjoy it!

Price Guide

Prices are based on admission costs for a family of four --- two adults and two children of paying age. Children 6 and under are free at some museums, but in most cases the age cutoff is 3.

$ $10 or less

$$ $11 to $20

$$$ $21 to $40

$$$$ More than $40

Table of Contents

I. The Great Outdoors
Page 11

Nature and Hikes · Farmers Markets
Farms and Dairies · Zoos and Animal
Parks   Family Camps · Fishing
Water Parks and Pools · Parks

II. DaVinci to DiMaggio
Page 63

Parks and Recreation · YMCAs
Boys and Girls Clubs
Sports Programs and Leagues
Scouts and Youth Development

III. Cultural Diversions
Page 79

Museums · Sites of Interest
Theater and the Arts · Arts
Participation

The Great Outdoors

With more than 300 days of sun each year and 10 months of divine weather (and hey, in July and August it's a dry heat, right?), the Valley is a picture-perfect place to relish the great outdoors.

In this section:

Nature and Hikes · Farmers Markets
Farms and Dairies
Zoos and Animal Parks
Family Camps · Fishing
Water Parks and Pools · Parks

Nature and Hikes

Since my family has moved back to the Valley we have gotten very interested in hiking. I have included here some of the easier and more popular trails, but if you find you want a more complete listing, an excellent resource are the guide books put out by the Arizona State Trails System. These books are available at Popular and REI sporting goods stores and are made to fit into a 3-ring binder. Each page details a hiking route, including information on difficulty, amenities and facilities.

Now, there is one thing I can't stress enough, so don't be surprised to find it written throughout this book: Don't forget the water. A lot of water.

Estimate what you think you will need and then double it.

In a climate as dry as ours it is easy to forget the need for water. Without humidity we don't sweat as much, so it takes longer for us to feel thirsty. But forgetting water is not just annoying, it is dangerous. So get in the habit of drinking a lot before and during every outdoor excursion, and get your kids in the habit, too.

Another important thing to remember, which is also discussed in the "Play It Safe" chapter, is the need for hikers to stay on the designated trails. For you or your child, getting off the trail and stepping on a jumping cholla cactus would be bad enough. Stepping on a diamondback rattler would be even worse.

"A" Mountain

Off Mill Avenue north of the ASU campus, Tempe

This hike is definitely best left for cool-weather months, as there is not much shelter or areas for rest on the way up. Still, though, it is a fairly short walk for folks with fairly short legs, and the payoff at the top --- the great view of ASU and Tempe --- makes it worth it. Best for ages 6 and up.

Desert Botanical Garden
1201 N. Galvin Parkway in Phoenix
480/941-1225
$$
Yes, the kids will actually like it. Even if they aren't interested in learning about plants per se, they will still enjoy the walk and the Hohokam artifacts. Bring a picnic lunch to enjoy at the tables, or buy something to eat there.

Boyce Thompson Arboretum
Highway 60, near Superior
520/689-2811
$$
Okay, okay, I know this is technically outside of the Valley. But it's such a great place to spend the day that I just had to include it. There are walking routes for every level and ability, picnic tables, a snack bar and a gift shop. The dog can come, too.

Squaw Peak Recreational Area
2701 E. Squaw Peak Drive
602/262-7901
Climbing to the top of Squaw Peak is a right of passage around here, but that doesn't mean that you have to do it on a Saturday. Mid-week excursions mean far fewer people and better parking. If you must visit the area on the weekend, consider hiking one of the less-mobbed trails.

Tonto National Forest
2324 E. McDowell Road
480/488-3441 or 480/379-6446
Within the forest, which runs east of the Valley
from US 60 up to Cave Creek, there are several
picturesque, easy hiking areas perfect for family
outings. Two of the best:

Cave Creek Trail #4
North of Cave Creek, on Spur Cross Road
This trail runs along Cave Creek (the actual creek,
not the town), and is considered perfect for·
beginning backpackers. More experienced hikers
won't be bored, though, as the trail is beautiful,
especially in the fall.

Lost Dutchman State Park
480/982-4485
off Highway 88 between Apache Junction and
Roosevelt Lake
$ fee per carload for day usage
You won't exactly feel like you've gotten away from
society when you visit Lost Dutchman State Park,
since it is an ever-popular spot for local picnickers
as well as snow birds in RVs and other campers just
passing through. Still, though, there in the shadow
of Red Mountain, this spot is one of the most
beautiful in the Valley. Most of the trails here are
short and easily managed, and all have markers to
identify various species of plants and cactuses.

Discovery Trail, for example, is a short loop --- only one-third of a mile. Jacob's Crosscut Trail is longer --- 6.5 miles --- but still an easy walk. In between are several more trails of varying lengths.

McDowell Mountains Regional Park
East of McDowell Mountain Road, north of Fountain Hills
602/506-2930
There are several beginner and moderate trails in this park, including Scout Trail #149 (one-third of a mile), and Gordon Wagner Memorial Trail (half a mile). On either of these you are likely to see plenty of wildlife in addition to all those plants and cactuses.

Papago Park Trail System
In Tempe, Between Curry and the 202, west of College Avenue (access at either east or west end)
602/350-5200
If you've never been to this system of trails, you may find it hard to believe that once you get there, you forget that you're smack-dab in the middle of town. But keep in mind that we're not talking lush greenery here. What's unique about this spot are the archeological sites, including Loma Del Rio, the remains of a seven-room Hohokam dwelling.

Papago Park/Hole in the Rock
Galvin Parkway and Van Buren
602/256-3220
Just north of the trail system listed above, Papago Park is where you will find the beautiful red "mini-mountains."

Black Canyon Campground
east of I-17 and north of the Carefree Highway
602/506-2930
This trail is a good distance --- two miles --- but nearly flat the whole way. Coded posts identify desert trees and shrubs.

Estrella Mountain Regional Park
south on Bullard Avenue to 143rd Drive
602/506-2930
The 2.86-mile Rock Knob Buggy Trail is another easy-but-beautiful one, where you're likely to encounter equestrians and enjoy mountain views. For a more challenging walk, continue south into the park and farther into the Sierra Estrella Mountains.

White Tank Mountain Regional Park
west on Olive Avenue, east of Glendale
623/935-2505
This area gets crowded on weekends, thanks to the

gorgeous 80-foot waterfall and numerous petro-glyphs. It is definitely worth seeing, though, as it is another of the handful of places where you can be so close to the city but feel so far away.

Usery Mountain Recreation Area
east of Usery Pass Road, north of Mesa
480/984-0032
$ fee per carload for daily use
Take a picnic, hike an easy trail such as the 1-mile Merkl Memorial, have a picnic and enjoy a panoramic view of the countryside. Again, there are plenty of trails to choose from based on your group's skills.

Indian Bend Wash Multi-Use Path
throughout Scottsdale, from Paiute Park through
McCormick Ranch Park
480/994-2526
Keep in mind when you start your walk that not only is this not a loop (the trail is a sort of lopsided "U" that meanders through the city), it is also not short (almost 12 miles). So you need to have transportation at some spot along the way or strong legs and time to kill --- or be riding a bike. Cyclists, skaters and joggers use this path, which cuts through several of the city's parks along Hayden Road.

Additional walking/hiking recreational areas

There are several other areas for hiking and walking around the Valley --- so many, in fact, that it would be next to impossible for you to run out of new areas to try during an October-through-April season of hiking.

Dreamy Draw Recreation Area
Phoenix Mountain Preserve
2421 E. Northern Avenue

North Mountain Recreation Area
Phoenix Mountain Preserve
10600 N. 7th Street
602/262-7901

Echo Canyon Recreation Center
Camelback Mountain area
E. McDonald Drive at Tatum Blvd.
602/256-3110
Keep in mind that few trails here are easy or quick.

Reach 11 Recreation Area
Union Hills Road and Tatum Boulevard
602/262-7797

South Mountain Park
10919 S. Central Avenue
602/495-0222 or 602/262-7393
The largest park around, South Mountain Park has plenty of stroller-friendly trails, as well as a great view from the top.

American Bicycle Association 602/961-1903

Scottsdale Bike System Map 480/312-2732

American Trails 520/632-1140
www.outdoorlink.com/amtrails/

Farmers Markets

The fare at each of these markets is varied, but expect fresh produce, baked goods, jams and jellies, gourmet foods and arts and crafts. Some close for the summer (June through late October), so you may want to call ahead.

Mesa Farmers Market
263 N. Center Street
480/644-2178
Friday mornings beginning at 8

Gilbert Heritage Farmers Market
Gilbert Historical Society parking lot (SW corner of Gilbert and Elliot Roads)
480/848-1234
Saturdays from 9 to 1

Town and Country Farmers Market
2021 E. Camelback Road in Phoenix
10 to 2 on Wednesdays

Scottsdale Farmers Market
The Borgata (Scottsdale Road between Lincoln and McDonald Drives)
480/998-1822
Friday afternoons from 1 to 6

Roadrunner Park Farmers Market
Roadrunner Park (Cactus Road and 35th Street)
Saturday from 9 to 1

Camelback Farmers Market
Vincent's Restaurant (3930 E. Camelback Road in Phoenix)
602/224-0225
Saturdays from 9 to 1

Patriots Square Marketplace

Patriot's Park (Washington and Central Avenues)
602/848-1234
Wednesdays from 10 to 2

Chandler Farmers Market

A.J. Chandler Park (Chandler Blvd. and Arizona Place)
480/782-2220
Tuesday afternoons from 3 to 7

Farms and Dairies

Awesome Big Bird Ranch and Incubator
Casa Grande
520/421-2002
$

Until recently, you only had to drive as far as
Chandler to get a look at ostriches being raised.
Alas, those days are gone, and now it requires an

hour's drive down to Casa Grande to experience these majestic (Well! Someone might find them majestic!) creatures. Big Bird is the largest ostrich ranch in the state, located on 330 acres. Now, in addition to seeing a slide show in which you will discover everything you ever wanted to know about ostriches but where afraid to ask, you will get to see computerized incubators, a talk about feathers and little ostrich families (known as breeding pairs). You can also feed ostrich chicks, buy ostrich gear (that is, stuff made *from* an ostrich, not *for* an ostrich) in the gift shop, and chow down on yummy ostrich-based food in the cafe, such as ostrich sloppy joes. Call ahead for tour schedule.

Crow's Dairy
10505 W. Broadway Road in Phoenix
623/936-4435
$$

This working dairy is now only open to large groups and school tours --- except for the last two weekends of October and the first two weekends of April. During those special-event weeks, visitors can enjoy interacting with the animals, hayride tours and a petting zoo. Proceeds benefit charity.

Dugan's Dairy Farm
2471 S. Dobson Road in Chandler (2 1/2 miles south
of Chandler Blvd.)
480/899-8795
$$

For folks living in the East Valley, Dugan's is the quickest route to a real farm experience. Keep in mind, though, that its tours are designed for school groups and field trips and not for individual families. There are farm animals to pet, and staff members will teach you how to milk a cow. Hayrides offer a tour of the facility, and at the end of your visit you get a free carton of milk.

Duncan's Family Farm
17203 W. Indian School Road
623-853-9880
$$
weekends only

If you are not familiar with the West Valley I guarantee you will start to look for the Arizona/California border as you head out toward Duncan's and the landscape gets flatter and more sparse. Don't turn around! In due time you'll see the Cotton Lane exit and the giant baby billboard on the north side of the highway. You're almost there.

For your gate fee, you will have the run of the place. There's a petting zoo, complete with themed areas such as the "Billy Goats Gruff" display and the "Charlotte's Web" pig paddock. The kids can ride the kiddie cow train, and the whole family can try its luck in the Arizona-shaped corn maze and purchase baked goods, jams, honeys and dressings at he bakery. During the farm's two featured annual events --- Pumpkin Fest in October and Corn and Melon Fest in June --- the crowds are large but the activities worthwhile. One of the most popular features of the farm is the U-Pick garden, 30 acres of berries, corn, beets, carrots, potatoes and other crops your family can pick and purchase by the bag.

The Duncans have been farming this corner of the Valley for generations, and opened up this small section in 1992 for school groups to see how a real farm works. Luckily for the rest of us, they expanded to accommodate the general public a few years later. Closed in July and August, Duncan's is open the rest of the year to school groups during the week and families on weekends.

Schnepf Farms
22601 E. Cloud Road in Queen Creek (9 miles south of Chandler Boulevard, off Rittenhouse)
480/987-3333
free; $$$ for special events
My husband grew up in Scottsdale and never knew that the far southeast Valley even existed. To him,

once you crossed over Guadalupe or headed east past Country Club, you might as well be in Globe. True, Schnepf (pronounced "Shneff") Farms is a bit of a hike. But that's part of it's charm.

This real, 600-acre working farm has been in the Schnepf family for more than 60 years. Since the mid-1970s, the Schnepfs have opened up much of it to the public from October through June. Any day of the week visitors can come and have a picnic, pet the goats and sheep or ride tricycles through the hay-bale race course (Anyone who doesn't think that that last one sound like fun hasn't seen my husband do it). There's also an organic pick-your-own garden, playground and a country store and bakery, where you can find homemade, pies, fudge, muffins, cookies, jams and salsa. On weekends, carousel and other rides are also available.

There are five annual events held at Schnepf. Every Thursday, Friday and Saturday evening in October is the farm's Pumpkin and Chili party; the Country Christmas Magic, complete with Santa, a reenactment of the Christmas story and a sleighbell hayride, is the second weekend in December. Arizona Day at the Farm is in March, the "Easter Eggcitement" celebration is in March or April, and the Peach Festival is in May. Schnepf's newest attraction is an October haunted house constructed around authentic sets from the movie "Three Kings."

Smith's Dairy

500 S. 99th Avenue in Tolleson
623/936-2363
free

This is a great place to visit in conjunction with Crow's, so that kids can see where the milk goes after it leaves the farm. Smith's is a real working dairy where the processing part of milk production is done. On a half-hour tour you will see where the bottles are set up and filled and where the milk is stored. Call ahead for tour schedules.

Youngs Farms

In Dewey (just outside Prescott, off I-17)
520/632-7272
free admission

You can pick up fresh produce, eggs, meat and cheeses at Youngs' Farm Store, eat homemade goodies at the restaurant and visit the "critter corral" petting zoo. There is also a plant nursery and craft area, and outdoor furniture for sale. Holiday turkeys are available, and Youngs hosts special events throughout the year. There is the Valentine Dinner and Moonlight Hayride in February, the Memorial Weekend Pie Festival and Antique Tractor Pull in May, the Garlic Festival in June, the Pumpkin Festival in October and other special dinners on most major holidays.

Zoos and Animal Parks

The local zoos are spread out across the Valley, and each has something different to offer. So, don't think that if you've seen one you've seen 'em all. Each has membership packages available, as well as special children's programs and unique animal interaction opportunities for all ages.

Out of Africa Wildlife Park
#2 N. Fort McDowell in Fountain Hills (2 miles north of Shea, off of the Beeline Highway)
480/837-7779
$$$
Undoubtably the most frustrating part of going to most zoos these days is the immense size of the

animal paddocks. "Did you get to see the lion/tiger/baboon/wolf?" "No, he was sleeping somewhere under a rock."

I can guarantee that that won't be the case at Out of Africa, where nearly every enclosure is accessible on all sides and the chain-link fence allows visitors to get within three feet of the animals. The park's focus is on two things: respect for the animals and interaction between them and people. The majority of what you will see are the big cats --- lions, panthers, leopards and several varieties of tigers. There are also bears, wolves, reptiles and other small animals, plus a playground, gift shop and a pretty impressive cafe. Out of Africa is a good size, too --- big enough so that you feel you've gotten your money's worth and small enough to easily see everything during your visit.

You absolutely will not want to miss the park's animal shows, which are held at scheduled times throughout the day. Crowd favorites --- especially for those with younger or not-so-attentive children --- are those that involve the lions and tigers: the Big Cat Show, Tiger Splash and the Cat Feeding. Various special events are held throughout the year, and in June through September the park has nighttime hours and special evening showtimes.

Superstition Reptile Exhibit
in Goldfield Ghost Town
4650 N. Mammoth Mine Road in Apache Junction
602/370-3266
$

Zack, the guy who runs the new and improved reptile extravaganza, really knows his stuff. This is someone who loves his job, and it shows. His enthusiasm for all things that slither and slink is infectious, actually, and you may leave with a new appreciation for snakes and gila monsters and lizards and scorpions and giant bugs.

From most spots in the Valley this is a pretty far drive, so you might want to save this trip for when you are already headed out to Goldfield, Roosevelt Lake, the Lost Dutchman State Park or some other far-East destination. Zack is constantly expanding, though, and soon he and his cold-blooded creatures will be worth the drive all by themselves.

World Wildlife Zoo
165th and Northern Avenues
623/935-WILD
$$$

Forgot your glasses? It doesn't matter at WWZ, where the animals are literally close enough to reach out and touch. You can feed a giraffe or an exotic bird, walk beneath a sleeping panther or stand toe-to-toe with a white tiger (separated by a chain-link fence in those last two cases). And don't think you will be sacrificing volume in exchange for proximity. On the contrary, the WWZ is a real zoo, where the state's largest collection of exotic animals is housed. While everyone has their personal favorite exhibit, most folks love the monkey islands. Because these animals are afraid of water, they don't need to be in cages and instead cavort on small lagoon-surrounded islands only a dozen feet or so from zoo visitors.

In addition to animal feedings and shows, patrons can ride a train through the hoofed-animal paddocks, ride the wild animal-themed carousel, visit the children's petting zoo or stroll through the aviary. The only animals you won't find are venomous reptiles, which is probably a good thing considering how close you are to them and they are to you.

Phoenix Zoo
455 N. Galvin Pkwy
602/273-1341
$$
What sets this zoo apart is its Harmony Farms area designed just for kids 9 and under. There have been days when my family has visited just this small area of the zoo and spent a couple of hours enjoying this small section of the zoo. Of course, there's a

whole lot more to see, including the section devoted to animals of Arizona, and baboons, tigers, lions, zebras, giraffes and other exotic animals in habitats that make it easy for visitors to see and hear. Personally, I have become a big fan of the otters. Catch them at a time when they're swimming around and you'll see why.

The zoo also has great summer programs for children, including Zoo Camp, in which participants learn what it is like to be a real zoo keeper.

Family Camps

Each spring, the local newspaper and Raising Arizona Kids magazine both come out with camp guides. Because there are so many overnight camps in Arizona, and day camps are numerous and ever-changing, I have not included a directory here and have instead listed web sites for camping organizations.

What is provided here is a listing of ranches and "Family Camps," that is, camps in Arizona that offer vacations for adults to do with their kids. These are great, usually inexpensive, family vacations in which parents and their kids can spend time together and select from a number of different activities to do alone or together.

Although all of these are in-state, there are many other family camps across the country. Some are specialty camps, offering classes in specific activities and sports, or educational and adventure opportunities in things like paleontology, space, river rafting or rock climbing. Again, contact the organizations listed below for additional information.

Also, check out the annual Summer Camp Expo for camps in the Valley, state-wide and beyond. The expo is usually held in February; the location varies. For information, call the **Western Association of Independent Camps** at the number listed below.

The American Camping Association
765/342-8456
Arizona office, ACA, 800/871-0270
www.acacamps.org

Kids Camps
www.kidscamps.com

The Camp Channel
www.campchannel.com

Western Association of Independent Camps
480/820-1702
www.waic.org

Chauncey Ranch/Sky Y
602/254-1571
Near Prescott

For one week near the end of its summer session, these Valley YMCA-run camps open their doors (and lakes and stables and mess halls) to families. You can do as much or as little as you would like to do. One thing to keep in mind: Cabins sleep 12, and if you have fewer than that in your family you most likely will be bunking with another family. But at these prices, you might not mind.

Triangle Y Ranch
520/884-0987
Near Tucson

Very similar to the Valley of the Sun Y's camps listed above but with one crucial difference: At Triangle Y, the cabins are divided into 4-bed rooms, so you won't be listening to some guy snoring all night. The price is slightly higher, but it's still a pittance. This camp offers weekend and weekly family camps.

Orme Summer Camp
520/632-7601
Mayer

One week at the end of each summer Orme holds its family camp, geared toward families with kids 16 and younger. There are crafts, sports and horsemanship.

The next two listings are for "guest ranches," which is a fancy way of saying "expensive family camps." Well, okay, there's a little more two it than that. But the upshot is, these are the spots to go when you want to leave behind the hustle and bustle of the city but not the comforts of home. Call for a brochure.

Lazy K Bar Ranch Camp
520/744-3050
Tucson
www.lazykbar.com

Tanque Verde Guest Ranch
520/296-6275
Tucson

Fishing

Arizona's Urban Fishing Program was launched in 1983 by the Game and Fish Department and some local cities. You need a $12 license if you are over 14. With it, each fisherperson can bring home a limit of four trout and four catfish each day. That's right --- trout and catfish! And you thought all those lakes had in them were giant Japanese goldfish!

For more information, call 602/942-3000 or check out www.gf.state.az.us.

Participating lakes:
Desert Breeze Lake
Chandler Blvd. and McClintock in Chandler

Water Ranch Lake
Guadalupe and Greenfield in Gilbert

Red Mountain Lake
Power and University in Mesa

Riverview Lake
Brown and Country Club in Mesa

Alvord Lake
Baseline and 36th Avenue in Phoenix

Cortez Lake
Dunlap and 35th Avenue in Phoenix

Desert West Lake
I-10 and 59th Avenue in Phoenix

Encanto Lakes
19th Avenue, north of the 202 in Phoenix

Papago Pons #1-3
Rural Road and McKellips in Phoenix

Chaparral Lake
Near Indian School and Hayden Roads in Scottsdale

Canal Lake
64th Street and the 202 in Tempe

Kiwanis Lake
Off Guadalupe, between Priest and Rural in Tempe

Water Parks and Pools

It shimmers like an oasis, the one spot on the horizon where waves of heat don't radiate upward into the parched sky. It's a given that the mercury will climb around here, beginning its ascent early in the spring and staying above 100 degrees until into October. That usually means more than five solid months of pool weather, which is great if you have a pool in your backyard, or if you can barter lawn care for pool usage with your neighbor. If not, though, never fear. Every community has its choice of swimming venues (don't forget to check out the YMCAs, listed in a later section), and usually they aren't as crowded as you might think.

Kiwanis Wave Pool

6111 S. All-America Way, Tempe (near Guadalupe and Mill Avenue in Tempe)
480/350-5201
$$

This huge pool has a water slide and 3-foot-high waves, and rents rafts and tubes. Because it is indoors, the Kiwanis Pool is open year-round --- and you won't get a sun burn.

The following water parks are all run by the same company and are all accessible by on the Web at www.golfland-sunsplash.com. All have numerous slides and attractions; call or visit the website for detailed information.

Big Surf

1500 N. McClintock Drive in Tempe (at Hayden)
480/947-7873
$$$$

Waterworld Safari Water Park

43rd Avenue and W. Pinnacle Peak Road in Glendale
(At Adobe Dam Recreation Area)
623/581-1947
$$$$

Sunsplash

155 W. Hampton in Mesa (US 60 and Country Club)
480/834-8319
$$$$

Pools

Chandler
Desert Oasis Aquatic Center,
1400 W. Summit Place (between Dobson and Alma
School, north of Elliot in Chandler)
480/732-1061 or 732-1062

Arrowhead Pool,
1475 W. Erie Street (between Alma School and
Dobson, north of Chandler Boulevard)
480/732-1064

Folley Pool
600 E. Fairview (between McQueen and Arizona
Avenue, off of Frye)
480/732-1063

West Chandler Aquatic Pool
250 S. Kyrene Road (1/2 mile south of Chandler
Blvd.)

Gilbert
Gilbert Municipal Pool,
on Burk, just south of Houston.
480/926-1030

Mesquite Aquatic Center,
on Mesquite, west of Gilbert Road
480/503-6292

Glendale

For information on Glendale facilities, call
623/930-2820

O'Neil Pool
6448 W. Missouri Avenue (near 65th Avenue and
Missouri)

Rose Lane Pool
5003 W. Marlette Avenue (near 51st Avenue and
Bethany Home)

Cardinal Pool at Glendale High School
6350 W. Glendale Avenue

Apollo Pool at Apollo High School
8045 N. 47th Avenue (at Northern)

Glendale Community College Pool
6000 W. Olive Avenue

Ironwood Pool at Ironwood High School
12603 N. 61st Avenue
(near Sweetwater and Cactus)

Cactus Pool at Cactus High School
15500 N. 63rd Avenue (at Greenway)

Litchfield Park
Litchfield Park Recreation
100 S. Litchfield Road
623/935-9040

Mesa
For more information on hosting events at Mesa
pools, call 480/644-2351.

Carson Junior High Pool
525 N. Westwood
480/644-2374
Also has a toddler pool.

Falcon Field Pool
4800 E. Falcon Field Drive
480/644-2375
Good pool for a party, since its features include
picnic tables, BBQ grills, ramadas and a sand
volleyball court.

Fremont Junior High pool
1001 N. Power Road
480/644-2369
Toddler pool here too.

44

Kino Junior High Pool
848 N. Horne
480/644-2376
Heated in the winter; has toddler pool.

Mesa Junior High
828 E. Broadway
480/644-2377
Has toddler pool.

Parkway Recreation Center
1753 E. 8th Avenue
480/644-2864

Poston Junior High Pool
2433 E. Adobe
480/644-2371
Toddler pool.

Powell Junior High
855 W. 8th Avenue
480/644-2378
Toddler pool here, too.

Rhodes Junior High pool
1860 S. Longmore
480/644-2550
Toddler pool.

Shepherd Junior High
1407 N. Alta Mesa Drive
480/644-3037
Zero-depth graduated entry, water slide, diving
area, sand volleyball court.

Stapley Junior High
3250 E. Hermosa Vista
480/644-4977

Taylor Junior High
705 S. 32nd Street
480/644-3036
Toddler pool, too.

Peoria

Peoria Municipal Swimming Pool
11200 N. 83rd Avenue

Phoenix

Alkire Pool
1617 W. Papago Street
602/261-8787

Cactus Pool
3801 W. Cactus Road
602/262-6680

Cielito Pool
4551 N. 35th Avenue
602/262-4752

Coronado Pool
1717 N. 12th Street
602/262-6709

Cortez Pool
3434 W. Dunlap
602/262-7107

Deer Valley Pool
19400 N. 19th Avenue
602/534-1842

Eastlake Pool
1548 E. Jefferson
602/261-8729

El Prado Pool
6428 S. 19th Avenue
602/261-8638

Encanto Pool
2125 N. 15th Avenue
602/261-8732

Falcon Pool
3420 W. Roosevelt
602/262-6229

Grant Pool
714 S. 2nd Avenue
602/261-8728

Harmon Pool
1239 S. 5th Avenue
602/261-8733

Hermoso Pool
5749 S. 20th Street
602/261-8731

Holiday Pool
4530 N. 67th Avenue
602/261-8031

Madison Pool
1440 E. Glenrosa
602/262-6494

Marivue Pool
5625 W. Osborn
602/261-8929

Maryvale Pool
4444 N. 51st Avenue
602/262-6685

Mountain View Pool
1104 E. Grovers
602/534-1347

Paradise Valley Pool
17648 N. 40th Street
602/534-5161

Perry Pool
3131 E. Windsor
602/262-7367

Pierce Pool
2150 N. 46th Street
602/262-6199

Roadrunner Pool
3502 E. Cactus Road
602/262-6789

Roosevelt Pool
6246 S. 7th Street
602/262-6832

Starlight Pool
7810 W. Osborn Road
602/495-2412

Sunnyslope Pool
301 W. Dunlap
602/262-7165

Telephone Pioneer Pool
1946 W. Morningside
602/495-2404

University Pool
1102 W. Van Buren
602/261-8730

Washington Pool
6655 N. 23rd Avenue
602/262-7198

Tempe
Clark Pool
1780 S. Roosevelt Street
480/350-5203

Escalante Pool
2150 E. Orange Drive
480/350-5204

Kiwanis Pool
6111 All America Way
480/350-5201

McClintock Pool
1830 E. Del Rio Drive
480/350-5202

Parks

Maybe one day you'll be across town on an errand and the kids will be getting a little restless in the back of the minivan and you'll all be in need of a little fresh air. Chances are, there's a park right around the corner that is just right for a 10-minute pit stop.

Or perhaps your 4-year-old's birthday is coming up and the thought of his entire preschool class convening in your dining room doesn't thrill you but you know he won't agree to a party at the same playground on the corner where he goes every day.

But a new, different, unexplored park with a duck pond and monkey bars instead of rings? Well, that's something else all together.

Originally I had listed every city park in the Valley. Then I happened to notice as I drove around one day that unfortunately, some of these parks were pretty awful. They were unsafe, unclean or otherwise un-recommendable. So instead, with the help of Parks and Rec officials in each city, I have chosen a few parks in each area of town that I can wholeheartedly endorse. Most of what you find listed below are larger parks, but keep in mind that each city has anywhere from six to several dozen smaller neighborhood parks as well.

Keep in mind that many of the larger, more well-equipped parks require reservations, fees or deposits for certain things such as ball fields and pagodas. If you are planning a big event it might be a good idea to call your city's parks department to check on availability and cost.

Telephone Pioneers of America Park
1946 W. Morningside in Phoenix
602/262-4543
This is the nation's fist barrier-free park for people with disabilities.

Chandler
480/782-2727

Arrowhead Meadows Park
1475 W. Erie Street

Desert Breeze Park
660 North Desert Breeze Blvd. East (Off McClintock, between Ray and Chandler)

Desert Oasis Park
1400 W. Summit Place

Fountain Hills
480/816-5152

Golden Eagle Park
Golden Eagle Blvd. (near Palisades)

Fountain Park
Saguaro Drive (at Palisades)

Four-Peaks Park
Del Cambre (at Four Peaks Elementary)

Gilbert
480/503-6200

Freestone District Park,
Lindsay and Juniper

Crossroads District Park,
Knox, west of Greenfield

Glendale
623/930-2820

Bonsall Park
59th Avenue and Bethany Home Road

Thunderbird Park
59th Avenue and Pinnacle Peak Road

Thunderbird Paseo
67th Avenue from Thunderbird to Greenway Roads

Mesa
480/644-2351

Gene Autry Park
4125 E. McKellips
(between Greenfield and Val Vista)

Greenfield Park
4105 E. Diamond (between Southern and Broadway)

Harmony Park
1434 S. 32nd Street (at US60)

Hermosa Vista Park
2255 N. Lindsay (north of McKellips)

Red Mountain Park
7745 E. Brown Road (east of Power)

Reed Park
1631 E. Broadway (west of Gilbert)
Dog-friendly.

Riverview Park
2100 W. 8th Street (at Dobson)
Dogs welcome here, too.

Skyline Park
Crismon and Pueblo
Come on over, Rover.

Peoria
623/773-7137

Sunnyslope Park
9180 N. 71st Avenue

Parkridge Park
9734 W. Beardsley Road

Windrose Park
8350 W. Windrose

Phoenix
602/262-6862 or the number listed

Cactus Park
3801 W. Cactus Road
602/262-6575

Cesar Chavez Park
35th Avenue and Baseline
602/262-6111

Cortez Park
35th and Dunlap Avenues
602/262-6575

Deer Valley Park
19602 N. 19th Avenue
602/495-3735

Desert Foothills Park

1010 Marketplace Way Southwest
602/534-2562

Desert West Park

6602 W. Encanto Blvd.
602/495-3700 or 262-4539

Encanto Park

15th Avenue and Encanto Blvd.
602/262-6412

Features **Enchanted Island**, an amusement-park area with 10 rides such as a carousel and ferris wheel. (For information on Enchanted Island, call 602/254-1200).

Margaret Hance Deck Park

67 W. Culver Street (near Central and McDowell)
602/534-2406

La Pradera Park

40th and Glendale Avenues
602/262-6575

Los Olivos Park

28th Street and Devonshire Avenue
602/256-3130

Maryvale Park
51st and Campbell Avenues
602/262-5030

Rose Mofford Sports Complex
9833 N. 25th Avenue

Moon Valley Park
7th Avenue & Coral Gables

Mountain View Park
7th and Cinnabar Avenues

Paradise Valley Park
17642 N. 40th Street
602/262-6696

Pierce Park
2150 N. 46th Street
602/534-1636

Roadrunner Park
3502 E. Cactus Road
602/262-6696

Starlight Park
78th Avenue and Osborn

Verde Park
9th and Polk Streets
602/262-6730

Scottsdale
480/312-2408

Vista Del Camino Park
7700 East Roosevelt (Roosevelt and Miller)
480-312-2330
Features the city's only off-leash dog run. For more info, call 312-2330 or 312-2783. Also has 18-hole disc golf course.

Scottsdale Ranch Park
10400 East Via Linda (104th Street and Via Linda)

Mountain View Park
8625 East Mountain View (Hayden and Mountain View)
480/312-2584

Horizon Park
15440 North 100th Street
480/312-2650

Eldorado Park
2311 North Miller Road (Miller and Oak)
480/312-2483

Chaparral Park
5401 North Hayden (Hayden and Jackrabbit)
480/312-2353

Cactus Park
7202 E. Cactus Road
Fitness Center Phone: 480/312-7967
Aquatics Center Phone: 480/312-7665

Tempe
For more information, call 480/350-5200

Clark Park
19th and Roosevelt Streets

Daley Park
Encanto Drive and College Avenue

Hollis Park
Dorsey Lane and Malibu Drive

Kiwanis Community Park
Mill Avenue and All-America Way (Baseline, south of Mill)

Papago Park
Curry Road and College Avenue

• • •

Skateboard Parks

Attention all you dudes who skateboard outside my video store: You don't have to mow down little children and old ladies (like me) anymore, because there are skateboard parks, for inliners and skateboarders such as yourselves:

Desert West Skateboard Plaza
67th Avenue and Encanto, between Thomas and McDowell in Phoenix
602/495-3700

Zone Skate Park
331 E. Dunlap in Phoenix.
602/861-9938
Admission

The Wedge at Eldorado Park
2311 N. Miller Road (at McDowell) in Scottsdale

Skyline Park
655 S. Crismon Road in Mesa

DaVinci to DiMaggio

Take your kid to parks and recreation classes or soccer practice and you can sit and talk with other adults! You'll meet new people and have grown-up conversations for a little while! And oh yeah, your children will burn off some of that extra energy, learn new skills and make some friends, too. It's a win-win situation for everyone involved.

In this section:
Parks and Recreation • YMCAs
Boys & Girls Clubs
Sports Programs and Leagues
Scouts and Youth Development

Parks and Recreation

These classes saved my sanity when I moved here and took the place of preschool for my two younger children. They are wonderful, either as one-shot holiday craft workshops, eight-week dance classes or even hiking excursions for adults. Prices vary but are reasonable.

Oh, and here's a little tip. You may find that some kids' classes fill up really quickly, so even if you are mailing your registration on the first possible postmark day, you aren't getting the classes you want. Someone clued me in on a little secret: mail your registration from the nearest regional post office, and mail it before the first pick up of the day. For example, if you life in Gilbert, the nearest big post office is in downtown Mesa.

Also, if you want a certain class and have over and over missed getting in, try registering for the fall session (ie, the one that registers in July for an August start date). With most P&Rs, this session is the slowest of the year.

Chandler 480/782-2727

Fountain Hills 480/816-5152

Gilbert 480/503-6200

Glendale 623/930-2820

Mesa 480/644-2351

Peoria 623/773-7137

Phoenix 602/262-6861 or 6862

Scottsdale 480/312-2408

Tempe 480/350-5200

YMCAs

Today's YMCA has great rates for family memberships, which entitle you to use the exercise rooms and classes and get discounts on sports and other kids' programs. In addition to offering after-school programs, most branches have a big choice of sports programs, too, including leagues for flag football and roller hockey along with old favorites such as T-Ball, soccer and basketball.

Ahwatukee Foothills
3233 E. Chandler Blvd.
480/759-6762

Chandler/Gilbert
1875 W. Frye Road
480/899-9622

Chris-Town
5517 N. 17th Avenue
602/242-7717

Glendale/Peoria
14711 N. 59th Avenue G
623/588-9622

Mesa
207 N. Mesa Drive
480/969-8166

Phoenix YMCA
Main Number: 602/528-5540 or 257-5120

Scottsdale/Paradise Valley
6869 E. Shea
480/951-9622

South Mountain YMCA
222 E. Olympia Drive
602/276-4246

Tempe
7070 S. Rural Road
480/730-0240

YWCA

The YWCA is focused on personal development, not sports, and runs programs for children and seniors. And the "W" stands for Women's, by the way.

Phoenix 602/258-0990
Valley West 623/931-7436

Boys & Girls Clubs

For a very nominal fee, the Boys & Girls Clubs give school-age children opportunities to meet new people and grow into a well-rounded adult. The Clubs' focus is on five areas: Character and Leadership; Education and Career Development; Health and Life Skills; the Arts; and Sports, Fitness and Recreation. Most programs are after school.

Gilbert 480/813-2020

Mesa 480/844-0963

Chandler 480/899-8302

Tempe 480/966-6656

Glendale 623/939-6952

Apache Junction 480/982-6381

Metro Phoenix 602/954-8182

Fountain Hills 480/816-1974

Scottsdale 480/860-5520

Sports Programs and Leagues

If you don't see a phone number for your area in the sport in which you are interested, call a neighboring chapter. For most sports, a good way to begin is with a YMCA or Parks and Rec class, which have shorter seasons and are less competitive. For other information, check the "Other Sports Leagues" section below.

Softball/Baseball

Chandler Girls Softball
480/963-7100

Paradise Valley Girls Softball League
602/997-8475

Chandler Youth Baseball
480/497-0026

Tempe Parks and Recreation Fall Instructional
Baseball Camp
480/350-5200

Little League

Little League is a national organization with dozens of chapters all over the Valley. All teams are included in the divisions listed, so call the appropriate number for more information or to be hooked up with a team in your area. Teams are organized by school district.

Rules mandate that children be at least 5 to play for a Little League team.

District 2
623/439-3261
Includes the West Valley.

District 3
602/971-7188
Includes Paradise Valley and Northeast Phoenix.

District 6
602/266-2055
Includes Fountain Hills, Scottsdale, Tempe and NW
Kyrene.

District 7
480/649-8587
Includes Mesa, Chandler and Gilbert

Soccer

Arizona Youth Soccer Association
602/433-9202

American Youth Soccer Organization
Glendale, Phoenix, Peoria 623/412-9500
East Mesa/Gilbert 480/830-9312
Dobson 480/814-8019

Mesa Soccer Club
480/507-0240

Football

Arizona Youth Football Federation (Pop Warner)
602/249-6747
Flag football for 7- and 8-year-olds; tackle football for 8- to 15-year-olds; cheerleading for 5- to 15-year-olds.

Hockey

Desert Youth Hockey Association
480/994-9119
www.dyha.org

Valley of the Sun Hockey Association
623/925-9686
Kids ages 4 to 18 from all over the Valley play for VOSHA, skating at the Ice House on McDowell and at Tower Plaza.

www.vosha.com

Castle Sports Club
11420 N. 19th Avenue
602/331-2582
Indoor roller hockey leagues

Casey at the Bat
Union Hills Drive and 40th Street in Phoenix
602/971-3224
In-line hockey leagues

The Rink-the-Rink North
19232 N. 38th in Phoenix
602/569-4459
1120 N. McClintock in Tempe
480/967-0405
In-line hockey leagues for kids and adults

Tennis

Arizona Tennis Association
480/970-0599
Offers lessons Valleywide

Arizona Youth Tennis Foundation
602/954-1414

Junior USA Tennis
Kiwanis Park Recreation Center
480/350-5730

Basketball

Basketball Congress International
602/252-6001
www.bcibasketball.org

Grand Canyon University Basketball Training
602/589-2789 or 602/589-2515
Camp in February for school-aged kids.

Golf

Junior Golf Association of Arizona
602/944-6168
www.jgaa.org

Other Sports Programs

Arizona Youth Sports (AYS)
602/843-0791
Basketball, soccer, T-Ball, baseball, softball and
flag football leagues for kids 4 to 13.

Chandler Rod and Gun Club
480/833-1909

Hunter Education Course for ages 10-14
Sponsored by the Arizona Game and Fish
Department
1-800-352-0700
www.gf.state.az.us

Arizona State Horsemans' Association
602/867-6814

Arizona Inline Skaters Association
602/962-6910

South Mountain Salvation Army
Offers programs in soccer, boxing, basketball, T-
Ball and volleyball.
602/276-7396

Little Little Dude Ranch Foundation
23803 N. 23rd Street (in the Pinnacle Peak area)
480/585-0463
A sports complex for kids 1 to 12. LLDR offers an
after-school golf program and camp, plus various
swimming activities.

Club Sar
4415 North Hayden (Hayden and Camelback)
480-312-2669
Run by the city of Scottsdale, Club Sar is a multi-sports instructional program for kids and adults. Renowned for its boxing program.

Arizona Sports Ranch Club and Training Center
19232 N. 38th Street in Phoenix
602/569-1457
Offers swim lessons and competitive teams, family fitness club memberships and summer day camp.

Scouts and Youth Development

Girl Scouts/Arizona Cactus Pine Council
602/253-6359

Boy Scouts of America/Grand Canyon Council
602/955-7747

Campfire Boys and Girls
602/954-7544
Campfire as it was explained to me by a very

patient representative, is a multi-program co-ed youth development agency --- sort of a roving Boys & Girls Club. There are six components: Club, which is a co-ed troupe similar to Girl or Boy Scouts; self-reliance, which is a curriculum-based prevention-education course; outdoor skills, which is a camp outreach for disadvantaged youth; teens in action (leadership development); and Camp, a low-priced summer day care. All programs are for kids 5 to 21.

4-H Youth Development
602/470-8086, extension 351

This ain't your father's 4-H. At least, it's not *my* father's 4-H, where his choices were raise a cow, raise a pig, raise a goat or raise a sheep (he chose to raise a pig, by the way). Sure, you can still raise animals --- the above-mentioned, plus small animals such as rabbits, poultry, cats and pigeons. There is also horsemanship training and wonderful dog-training projects in which students can ready a dog for use by someone who is blind, deaf or uses a wheelchair. There are programs in arts and crafts, computers, science, public speaking, volunteerism, nutrition, leadership, money skills, babysitting and even garbology. 4-H, which stands for Head/Heart/Hands/Health, is open to kids 4 to 19.

Cultural Diversions

Museums are more than big, quiet buildings with old paintings on the wall, and the symphony does not have to put anyone to sleep. Even most of the fine art museums in the Valley have special programs just for children.

In this section:

Museums • Sites of Interest
Theater and the Arts • Arts
Participation

Museums

Arizona Doll & Toy Museum
602 E. Adams Street
602/253-9337
$
About 200 dolls from as far back as the 1700s are on display. Best for kids 8 and older. There are other places of interest within Heritage Square (602/262-5071 for info), including historic homes, but most of it is not suitable for children.

Arizona Hall of Fame Museum
1101 W. Washington
602/255-2110
free
A small museum featuring an ever-changing array of exhibits on interesting Arizonans that most of us have probably never heard of. Past exhibits have featured the Navajo Code-Talkers, a group of men who used their native language to develop a secret code used during World War II by the United States government; and the Buffalo Soldiers, a group of African-American fighting men from our state. Generally, this museum is best for kids 9 and up, but with the right level of parental interaction, even younger children will get something out of it.

Arizona Historical Society Museum at Papago Park

1300 W. College Avenue (College and Weber)
480/929-0292
free; donations welcomed

This museum is a hard-floor-and-high-ceilings kind of place, where pounding feet echo. It is fascinating, though, and the very best place to learn about the development of Central Arizona and the Valley through 1,100 years of history. Some exhibits are permanent and others change, but all educate in an interesting way. Any kid who is at least 6 and has a good attention span will get a lot out of his or her visit here. Summer programs are available for children; for information ask for extension 137.

Arizona Military Museum

52nd Street, just north of McDowell
602/267-2676
free; donations welcomed

If your kid is fascinated with uniforms and metals and weapons, this is the place for you. Displays begin with the Conquistadors in 1540 and go through Desert Storm in the early nineties. There are interactive exhibits, including an honest-to-goodness Vietnam veteran Huey helicopter in which visitors can sit and pretend to man the controls. Outside the museum is a very large display of military vehicles. This museum has very limited hours, so call before you go.

Hoo-Hoogam Ki Museum
10005 E. Osborn Road in Scottsdale
480/850-8190
free; donations welcomed

This museum is devoted to the study of the Pima and Maricopa Indian tribes. The snack bar features authentic fry bread and other Indian fare, and the museum itself is interesting to even the youngest children.

Arizona Mining and Mineral Museum
1502 W. Washington
602/255-3791
free; donations welcomed

The folks at this museum say it's best for kids at least 8 years old, which is understandable considering the subject matter. It's a good spot to go to in conjunction with a visit to other downtown museums. Still, though, the Mineral Museum does have some interesting exhibits, like yummy-looking meals made entirely of rocks.

Arizona Museum for Youth
35 N. Robson Street in Mesa
480/644-2467
$

A small museum with plenty of hands-on exhibits for kids who are at least 3 or 4. What's great about this place, besides the price, is that its layout and

size prevent you from losin
Check out the museum's
programs, too.

Arizona Railway
399 N. Delaware Street in
480/821-11
free; donations welcomed

The small indoor section of this museum showcases memorabilia dating back to the early years of the railroad. What kids like best, though, are the giant engines displayed outside the museum. Because it is entirely run by volunteers, the museum has very limited hours.

Arizona Science Center
600 E. Washington
602/716-2000
$$$

This place is best enjoyed one-on-one, if possible, and at off-peak hours. There are so many things to see and do that it is easy to get overwhelmed and end up doing everything half-way or to walk around aimlessly and do nothing at all. But with one parent and one kid (4 years old at the very least, but there is no upper end of the age spectrum), it is possible to formulate a game plan and stick to it. Everything is very hands-on at the Science Center, of course, and it is one of those rare places where kids learn

...st. Try to see the Planetarium if ...me, the extra money and a child who ... or 8.

Arizona State Capitol Museum
1700 W. Washington Street, first floor
602/542-4675
free; donations welcomed

Did you know that the official state reptile is NOT the gila monster, as I would have guessed, but is instead the Arizona Ridgenose Rattlesnake? (The ringtail cat, of course, is the official state mammal). We've got 12 official state symbols, in fact --- more than any other state. In addition to learning all about our symbols, kids can see a wax figure of the state's first governor, as well as other bits of history set up just as it was when Arizona became a state in 1912. Exhibits are designed for fourth graders, so kids 8 to 11 would be best-suited for this museum.

Buckhorn Wildlife Museum
5900 E. Main in Mesa
480/832-1111
$

Get up close and personal with the animals of Arizona. This museum feature stuffed and mounted examples of everything that slithers, slinks, crawls, flies or bounds its way across the Grand Canyon State.

Buffalo Museum of America
10261 N. Scottsdale Road in Scottsdale
480/951-1022
$
Children of all ages are welcome to come learn about these giant furry beasts, some of which have been stuffed and saddled for great photo opportunities. (Note to animal-rights activists: These animals were already dead when the museum stuffed and saddled them).

Cave Creek Mistress Gold Mine and Museum
14 miles north of Cave Creek in Carefree; 1.6 miles on gravel road after pavement ends, on the left-hand side
480/488-0842
$ For tours; area exploration free; donations welcomed.
This is on the side of a mountain, and it is a mine, for goodness sake, so this isn't a place to set 'em loose and take a nap. Lots of services and kids workshops are offered, so you might want to call

ahead and make a day --- or a weekend --- of it. And don't forget to bring a carrot for Gabby the donkey.

Champlin Fighter Aircraft Museum
480/830-4540
$$

This museum is called "the Smithsonian of fighter aircraft," with three large hangars full of internationally designed planes dating back to World War I. Tours are available.

Confederate Air Force Museum
Northeast corner of Greenfield and McKellips in Mesa
480/924-1940
$$

This museum is right next to Champlin, adjacent to Falcon Field, and showcases World War II memorabilia, including aircraft and newspapers. A dozen planes are on display here.

Desert Caballeros Western Museum
21 N. Frontier Street in Wickenburg
520/684-2272
$$

At some point in your family's life you will almost certainly be gripped with the urge to take a day trip to Wickenburg. When you do, make sure that the Desert Caballeros Western Museum is on your agenda. Best for kids 4 and up, this museum focuses on the late 1800s' settlement of the Wickenburg area through period rooms, with authentic furniture, clothing and toys and a general store replica. There is a western-town street scene downstairs, a diorama, and changing exhibits of cowboy gear and the like.

Deer Valley Rock Art Center
3711 W. Deer Valley Road
602/582-8007
$$

This nature preserve and anthropology museum contains a couple thousand Native American petroglyphs from dozens of tribes. There are some children's activities, such as a petroglyph scavenger hunt; best for children age 3 and up.

Fleischer Museum

17207 N. Perimeter Drive, Scottsdale
480/585-3108
free; donations welcomed

American Impressionist art is on display year-round at this museum. It's a great place to take your kids ... if they love American Impressionist art. If not, you might want to think twice about bringing them here until they are old enough to appreciate it and quiet enough to let others do so, too.

Hall of Flame Firefighting Museum

6101 E. Van Buren (near Priest Drive)
602/275-3473
$$

The world's largest firefighting museum, the Hall of Flame displays everything imaginable related to fire service. There are helmets and coats and patches and more than 130 firefighting vehicles representing five continents and covering 300 years. A member of the National Historical Fire Foundation, this museum lets kids (and their parents) try on gear and climb aboard a real fire
s-on activities let children
'n about fire safety.

Halle Heart Center

2929 S. 48th Street in Tempe (north of Southern)
602/414-5353
free; donations welcomed

The Halle Heart Center is an interactive museum geared toward kids 8 to 11 that was built entirely with donations. Several different centers allow children to learn about the human heart, of course, and the ways they can keep their own hearts healthy and strong.

Heard Museum

2301 N. Central Avenue (north of McDowell)
602/252-8848
$$

With a focus on native art and artifacts, this 10-gallery museum features ancient and modern exhibits by and about Native Americans. There are a lot of things to do, including weaving your own baskets. You might find that this museum is best for kids who are 7 and older. Heard also has a north location at the El Pedregal Festival Marketplace at Scottsdale Road and Carefree Highway (480/488-9817), but that spot offers no interactive exhibits and is definitely an adult-geared kind of place.

Mesa Southwest Museum
53 N. Macdonald
480/644-2230
$$
Housed here are the state's largest collection of dinosaurs (the animated, mechanical variety), as well as 1,000-year-old Indian petroglyphs, pottery and fossils. The dinosaurs might be scary to kids under 6. There are classes and workshops throughout the year for children.

Petersen House Museum
NW corner of Southern Avenue and Priest Drive
480/350-5151
free; donations welcomed
A Queen Anne Victorian home built in 1892, the Petersen House is run by the Tempe Historical Society and gives visitors a glimpse into life in early 1900s' Phoenix. The staff recommends that children be at least elementary-age.

Phoenix Art Museum
1625 N. Central Avenue (at McDowell)
602/257-1222
$$; free on Thursdays
Because of the depth and breadth of the exhibits at the Phoenix Art Museum, it is not a place where children usually get bored. The "Family Gallery" is

geared specifically at children as young as age 4, which is also the age at which kids can begin taking classes and workshops. This is a great place to begin to encourage arts appreciation in your child.

Phoenix Family Museum
602/253-0501
Set to open in 2003, this museum will until its opening stage mobile exhibits around the Valley and accept help from interested volunteers.

Phoenix Museum of History
105 N. 5th Street
602/253-2734
$$

From the lobby, the Museum of History looks to be on the small side. You'll be amazed, though, at how much there is to experience inside the exhibit area. My family's favorite activity is loading the wagon, in which we pretend we are pioneers trekking west across the prairie. We sort through the three dozen or so labeled blocks and try to prioritize what to take with us in the little wooden wagon. It is fun to see how priorities have changed as the girls have gotten older; the first time we tried this, they insisted on loading the sugar, candy and toys first and didn't see the need for an extra wagon wheel or water (deciding that we could just stop for Slurpees along the way). The next time we went, though, nearly three years later, they had a much better sense of why soap would be important, and they even made room for Daddy's coffee. Because most of the exhibits are unchanging, this is someplace to go every couple of years; as they get older, your children will get more and more out of the experience. The museum provides activity sheets for the kids, which really added to my 4-year-old daughter's enjoyment.

Phoenix Police Museum

SE corner of Central and Jefferson
602/534-7278 (PAST)
free; donations welcomed

I love this place. It's not too big, the information is fascinating, and there is something of interest for every age. The kids can try on police equipment while their parents read about the Trunk Murderess and all those other sick, twisted criminals in the state's history. Is it just me, or does the criminal element in this state seem a whole lot more deranged than those who commit their crimes elsewhere? Spend some time at this museum (or just read the newspaper ...) and I'm sure you'll agree.

Pueblo Grande Museum
4619 W. Washington Street
602/495-0900 or 0901
$

I have a feeling that this place --- a 1,000-year-old historical landmark --- could fast become my oldest daughter's home away from home. She and other budding archeologists will love it here, where for a very nominal fee they can tour a Hohokam village ruin and take part in several hands-on, interactive activities. Best for kids who are 6 and older; summer classes and workshops for kids who are at least 8.

Shemer Art Center
5005 E. Camelback Road (at Arcadia)
602/262-4727
free; donations welcomed

This is not a shut-up-and-look-at-the-paintings kind of place. Even very young children are welcome here and should enjoy the colonial dollhouse on permanent display and the sculpture garden. Occasionally the museum features exhibits specifically geared to children, and summer art classes are available for children 4 and up.

Telephone Pioneer Museum

20 E. Thomas Road (NW corner of Thomas and 2nd
Street, in the U.S. West Building)
602/630-2060
free

Open by appointment only, this museum will show
your kids what life was like when telephones had
dials ... and even before. There are some hands-on
activities and exhibits on everything phone-related
since Alexander Graham Bell.

West Valley Art Museum

17420 N. 114th Avenue in Surprise
623/972-0635
$

Children of all ages are welcome, and certain events
and exhibits throughout the year are geared
specifically toward them, so call first and see
what's going on.

Regional Museums

Okay, I admit that I am a history buff, but I do think that everybody will find something interesting at their town's museum. As for the kids, it's probably best to catch them when they're old enough to have a decent attention span but not so old that they balk at doing anything they suspect might have some educational value. So we're talking 6- to 9-year-olds, give or take. The following museums each concentrate on their city or town's history and development, frequently with exhibits on early settlement and founding families, education, clothing and changes over the years. Typically, these museums are free but thrilled with donations.

Mesa Historical Museum
2345 N. Horne
480/835-7358

Peoria Historical Museum
10304 N. 83rd Avenue
623/487-8030

Tempe Historical Museum
809 E. Southern Avenue
480/350-5100

Scottsdale Historical Museum
7333 E. Scottsdale Mall
480/945-4499

Chandler Historical Museum
178 E. Commonwealth Avenue
480/786-2842

Gilbert Historical Museum
10 S. Gilbert Road
480/926-1577

Cave Creek Museum
6140 E. Skyline Drive
480/488-2764

Glendale Historical Society Manistee Ranch House
51st and Northern Avenues
623/435-0072

Superstition Mountain Historical Society/Lost Dutchman Museum
Goldfield Ghost Town, Apache Junction
480/983-4888

Buckeye Museum
116 E. Highway 85
623/386-4333

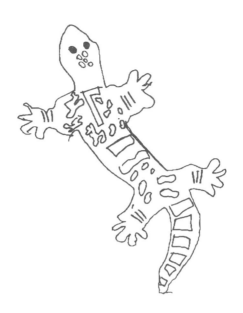

Sites of Interest

Pioneer Arizona Living History Museum
I-17, Exit 225 (12 miles north of Bell Road)
623/465-10⁻⌐
$$

Get a feel for how life was iⁿ
ago as you walk through the I
buildings, including a sheriff
and Victorian home are autl
or painstakingly restore(
working blacksmith's shop a

their wares to the public, plus a restaurant, live shows and even a 500-pound pig named Harold (our family's favorite, even though all he did was sleep and snore loudly when we paid a visit). Call for information on upcoming events, and make sure when you go that you stock up on water before you start out on your tour. Other tips: go on weekends in the fall and winter when it is cooler and there is more happening, bring a wagon or all-terrain stroller for babies, toddlers or preschoolers, and watch out for rattlesnakes. Seriously --- this out-of-the-way spot of desert is where these guys feel most at home.

Tovrea Castle
4633 E. Van Buren Street in Phoenix
602/261-8699

Yes, it looks really cool from the outside, but inside it's really just a round house. Recently renovated for public tours by the Historic Preservation Society, Tovrea has long enchanted everyone driving by on Van Buren. How, we've wondered, does the family dog negotiate all those cactuses? Older kids might appreciate the tour, but the little ones might be best left to use their imaginations regarding what goes on up on the hill.

Cosanti

6433 Doubletree Ranch Road in Paradise V
480/948-6145

This very unique structure blends dese
landscaping and earthformed concrete architectural
structures. It is a smaller version of Arcosanti
near Cordes Junction (602/254-5309 for
information on Arcosanti).

Mystery Castle

800 E. Mineral Road in Phoenix
(In the Foothills of South Mountain Park, 2 miles
south of Baseline Road)
602/268-1581
$$

Mystery castle was built around 1940 by Boyce
Luther Gulley as a sort of life-sized desert sand
castle for his daughter, who now conducts tours of
the 18-room, antique-filled structure.

Goldfield Ghost Town/Superstition Scenic Railroad

4 miles north of Apache
480/98
$$ for the railroad
Once you get to Goldfield y
activities, including panni
riding, a 20-minute train ri
tour of the mine or museum.

t town of Tortilla Flat

rtheast of Apache Junction
on Highway 88
480/984-1776

s a population of 6, with a
:am shop and post office. I guess
ᴛᴎᴇ workforce commutes in. The town is just a few minutes past Goldfield, so you probably want to see both on the same day.

Rawhide Western Town
23023 N. Scottsdale Road in Scottsdale
480/502-1880

There is a definite educational aspect to this theme park, designed to resemble an Old West town. Mostly, though, Rawhide is for fun, with comedy and outlaw shows, panning for gold and a petting zoo. There are several special events held there throughout the year; call for a calendar or information on what's coming up.

Fountain Hills fountain

It's recognized as the world's tallest fountain by
e folks at Guinness. You don't need directions to
it; the 560-foot tall jet of water shooting in
should show you the way. If you go to see
mind that it only runs for 15 to 30
e hour, from 9 to 9.

Luke Air Force Base
7383 N. Litchfield Road in
623/856-6012
free; donations welcomed
Best for 4th grade and up, the tour of this base is
pretty extensive and great for budding flight buffs.

Sahuaro Ranch Park
9802 N. 59th Avenue (Two miles north of downtown
Glendale)
623/939-5782
This 16-acre homestead is a beautiful pace to tour
or just watch the strolling peacocks. It features
seven original buildings, plus a milkhouse and
blacksmith shop. Tours are offered only on certain
days of the week, so call ahead.

Tempe Town Lake
480/517-4050
Along the 202, between Mill Avenue and McClintock
Rent a kayak, canoe or paddleboat, or if you've got
really strong legs, walk arc
growing array of things to
the Valley's newest tourist

Theater and the Arts

The League of American Theatres and Producers

1-888-BROADWAY

Call this toll-free line for information on every touring Broadway show across the country. You can get the low-down on locations, times, prices and plot synopses.

West Valley Fine Arts Council
623/935-6384
Call for a calendar of children's and family events.

Ballet Arizona
602/381-1096

Civic Plaza Box Office
602/262-7272
Tickets available for performances at the Orpheum Theater, the Herberger and some at Symphony Hall.

Chandler Theater for the Arts
250 N. Arizona Avenue
480/782-2680
Call for information on upcoming events.

Symphony Hall Box Office
602/495-1999
Several family concerts are performed throughout the year, including the Phoenix Suns Family Concert Series for kids 6 to 12. That Sunday series runs from October through April.

Childsplay
480/350-8101

Childsplay usually puts on nine or ten performances a year at the Herberger, the Tempe Performing Arts Center or the Scottsdale Center for the Arts, plus various school locations. Recent shows have included "The Wind in The Willows," "The Velveteen Rabbit" and "And Then They Came for Me." Call for a brochure, which gives information on each performance and includes age recommendations. All shows are geared toward children who are at least 4, but some are more appropriate for older children. "Season Sampler" ticket packages are available for families who plan to attend a few shows each season.

Civic Plaza Box Office
602/262-7272

Kids Connection
623/930-3530

Performances for children at the Glendale Public Library by a high-school troupe.

Herberger Theater Center
222 E. Monroe Street in Phoenix
602/252-8497

The venue for six different companies, including Childsplay, Center Dance Ensemble, Arizona Jewish

Theatre, the Actors' Theater of Phoenix and
Arizona Theater Company (which can also be reached
at 602/256-6995).

Desert Stages, Inc.
8473 E. McDonald Drive in Scottsdale
480/483-1664
Family entertainment; children 3 and up can
audition.

Grady Gammage Memorial Auditorium
ASU campus in Tempe
480/965-3434
The venue for dozens for plays, musicals and other
shows throughout the year.

Mesa Little Theatre
Mesa Arts Center 155 N. Center Street
Box Office: 480/644-2560
Various performances throughout the year, some
family-oriented.

Mesa Symphony Orchestra
480/897-2121
Plays at the Chandler Center for the Arts and other
sites in the East Valley.

Red River Music Hall
730 N. Mill Avenue in Tempe
480/829-OPRY (6779)
Annual family-friendly performance in December.

Scottsdale Symphony Orchestra
3817 N. Brown Avenue
480/945-8071
Performs at Scottsdale Center for the Arts and Desert mountain High School Auditorium.

Theater League
602/952-2881
Call for info on road companies touring in and around the Valley.

Arts Participation

Theater Works
9850 W. Peoria Avenue in Peoria
623/815-1791 (info) or 623/815-7930 (tickets)
Numerous workshops and kids' programs for all ages and experience levels, plus a number of performances.

Valley Youth Theater
525 N. 1st Street (at Fillmore)
602/253-8188
Workshops and performances for children.

The Imagination Corporation/Discovery Dance
ASU Department of Theater
480/965-2661
Classes for children in grades 1-6.

Girls Chorus of Scottsdale
480/348-2787
For girls 7 to 18 years old, the Chorus practices weekly and performs six concerts each year. Scholarships are available to some members. Call the number above for concert or audition information.

Phoenix Boys Choir
602/264-5328
Call for performance information, or for info on auditions for boys 7 to 12.

Phoenix Girls Chorus
602/252-5562

Performances throughout the year; auditions held when there are openings.

Phoenix Children's Chorus
602/534-3788 or 480/961-5191

Phoenix Symphony Guild Youth Orchestra
602/277-7013

Metropolitan Youth Symphony Mesa
480/456-9501

Auditions for students through ninth grade are held each September for this orchestra, which practices in Mesa and holds nearly all of its performances in the East Valley. Usually the MYSM performs about four shows a year; call for ticket information.

Mesa Youtheatre
155 N. Center Street
480/644-2681 (info) or 480/644-2560 (box office)

Performances, classes, workshops, camps, troupes; "Technical Difficulties" program teaches kids different aspects of theater production.

Performing Arts Series for Children,

Community Services Department of Tempe
Edna Vihel Center for the Arts, 3340 S. Rural Road
480/350-5287
Saturday programs and workshops.

Vagabond Youth Theater
602/499-1018

West-Valley-focused theater group, with workshops, classes and summer apprenticeships in every field of the theatre. Up to two shows a year for children.

Greasepaint Scottsdale Youtheatre at Stagebrush Theater

7020 E. 2nd Street in Scottsdale (at Goldwater)
480/661-4180

Classes, workshops, summer camps and a half-dozen or so annual performances in which all the actors are children. A very professional troupe that acts as a springboard for many talented young performers hoping to make it in the theatre. Open auditions are held for kids 6 and up.

Phoenix Theater's Cookie Company
100 E. McDowell (at Central)
602/254-2151

Weekend performances October through May,

complete with cookies and milk, for 3- to 10-year-olds. Also workshops and a summer academy for 3- to 17-year-olds. For academy or audition information, call 602/258-1974.

PlayWright's Theatre
1121 N. 1st Street
602/253-5151
www.primenet.com\pwt

Workshops and performance opportunities for children and adults. This company covers all aspects of theater, beginning with the writing process.

Fountain Hills Community Theater
480/837-9661

Workshops, summer theater camp and two children's productions annually. Call for performance and audition information.

The Playhouse Theatre for Children
Peoria
623/487-9434

Auditions for children 8 and up; five performances a year for children.

Great Arizona Puppet Theater
602/262-2050
302 W. Latham Street in Phoenix
azpuppets.org

Shows throughout the year for kids from preschool through 6th grade.

The Phoenix Center for Community Arts
214 E. Moreland (near 3rd Street and McDowell)
602/262-4627

Cultural and performing arts. Metals, photography, ceramics. Fine arts, toddler, mommy and me. Classes in performing arts, music, dance. Artist-in-residence program. Toddler to 18. Call for catalog.

Same Time Next Year

Annual Festivals and Events

The first few months after my family moved here we hit Gilbert Days, the Chocolate Festival in Glendale, the Chandler Ostrich Festival, the Fiesta Bowl Parade and the MAMA Festival in Tempe. They were each very different from one another, pretty inexpensive (well, free, if you've got the will power to avoid buying kettle corn or tickets to the ostrich races or *chocolate*, for goodness sake), and wonderful, exhausting entertainment for the kids.

It's a good idea to check with the listed festival numbers or Chambers of Commerce a month or so before the event you're interested in is scheduled to occur, as dates may change slightly. This is especially true of some of the expos, sporting events and trade shows listed.

While we're on the subject, you might want to take the opportunity to create your own family's "Same Time Next Year" traditions. At our house, the last Saturday in September is "Sister-Brother Day," in which the kids make cards for each other and plan a day's activity for the whole family. Your family could set out to have a picnic on a certain day each month

Most of the events are free, but the expos and trade shows usually charge an entrance fee.

Scottsdale Chamber of Commerce
480/945-8481

Apache Junction Chamber of Commerce
480/982-3141

Buckeye Town Hall
623/386-4691

Carefree/Cave Creek Chamber of Commerce
480/488-3381

Chandler Chamber of Commerce
480/963-4571

Fountain Hills Chamber of Commerce
480/837-1654

Gilbert Chamber of Commerce
480/892-0056

Glendale Special Events and Tourism
623/930-2960

Goodyear City Information
623/932-2171

Mesa Chamber of Commerce
480/969-1307
Tourist Information 480/827-4700

Peoria Chamber of Commerce
623/979-3601

Phoenix Chamber of Commerce 602/254-5521
Area Information 480/945-1191
Convention and Visitors Bureau 602/254-6500
www.arizonaguide.com
Tourist Hotline 602/252-5588

Surprise/Northwest Valley Chamber of Commerce
623/583-0692

Tempe Chamber of Commerce
480/967-7891

Tolleson Chamber of Commerce
623/936-5070

January

Arizona National Boat Show and Fishing Expo
Memorial Colosseum
602/277-4748
$$

Fiesta Bowl
480/350-0900
Prices vary

Most activities, including the parade, band competition and, of course, the football game, begin New Year's Eve weekend.

Art of Fun Fest
Scottsdale Stadium
602/488-2014

An arts and crafts festival with food vendors, entertainment, live music and children's activities.

Martin Luther King Jr. Celebration
Phoenix
602/256-3133

Arrowhead Kennel Club Dog Show
Peoria Sports Complex
623/773-7137

Parada Del Sol
Scottsdale
480/990-3179

One of the biggest, most longstanding parades in the Valley.

PRCA Rodeo (Formerly the Old Timers' Rodeo)
Phoenix
602/258-8568
$$$

Southwest Fest
Rawhide in Scottsdale
602/488-2014
Arts and crafts festival.

Quartzsite Pow Wow
520/927-6325

Scottsdale Celebration of Fine Arts
480/443-7695

Trash & Treasure Sellebration
Heritage Square in Phoenix
602/262-5029
Rummage sale to raise money for Heritage Square.

West Valley Native American Indian Festival
Litchfield Park
623/932-2260 or 935-6384

Glitter and Glow
Downtown Glendale
623/930-2960
On the last night of the Glendale Glitters holiday light festival, all of downtown is lit up, including a number of hot-air balloons that line the downtown streets.

February

Sahuaro Ranch Antique Tractor Show
Sahuaro Park in Glendale
623/939-5782
A celebration of 19th- and 20th-century technology, with tractor and engine displays, historic homes tours and an apple pie contest.

All Arabian Horse Show
Westworld in Scottsdale
480/515-1500

Arizona Renaissance Festival
(weekends through March)
Apache Junction
520/463-2700

Arizona Senior Olympics
various locations around the Valley
602/261-8765

Have a Heart Fest
Peoria Stadium
602/488-2014
Usually held Valentine's weekend, this arts and crafts festival sponsors a blood drive to benefit the local blood bank.

Matasuri (A Festival of Japan)
Heritage Park in Phoenix
602/262-5071
This festival highlights Japanese culture and includes authentic food, crafts, art and children's activities. There are martial arts demonstrations, Taiko drums and folk dances.

Territorial Days
480/644-2230
Old West celebration held in downtown Mesa, with children's activities, music, food and demonstrations.

Chinese Week
Phoenix
602/534-3751

High Desert Fest
Carefree Highway at I-17
602/488-2014
Arts and crafts festival.

Peoria Street Fair
Peoria Sports complex
623/773-7137

Cowboy Winter Range
Ben Avery Shooting Range
623/582-8313
One of many special shooting (and archery) competitions held at Ben Avery during the year.

Drag Racing Nationals
Firebird International Raceway in Chandler
480/268-0200

Fountain Hills Great Fair
480/837-1654
Arts and crafts festival sponsored by the Chamber of Commerce.

Peoria Arts and Crafts Festival
Peoria Sports Complex
623/773-7137

Goodyear Rodeo Days
623/932-2260

Chandler Greek Festival
480/899-3330

Fan Fest
Peoria Sports Complex
623/773-7137
Stadium tours, baseball card show, player autographs and a youth clinic.

Helz-A-Poppin Days Rodeo
Buckeye
623/386-2727

World Championship Hoop Dance Contest
Heard Museum in Phoenix
602/252-8840

Lost Dutchman Days and Rodeo
Apache Junction
480/982-3141

O'odham Tash, Indian Pow Wow & Rodeo
Casa Grande
520/836-4723

Parada Del Sol Rodeo
Rawhide in Scottsdale
480/990-3179

Northwest Black History Month Celebration
Peoria Municipal complex
623/773-7137
Food, music, vendors, children's activities and educational displays.

Renaissance Festival of Arizona
Apache Junction
520/463-2700
Weekends through March

Scottsdale Fine Arts and Chocolate Festival
480/837-5637

Annual Spring Grand American Trap Shoot
Phoenix Trap & Skeet Club
623/935-2691

Wickenburg Gold Rush Days & Rodeo
520/684-5479

Winter National Rifle Shoot
Ben Avery Shooting Range
623/582-8313, extension 0

Glendale Chocolate Affaire
623/930-2996
Arts and crafts, food and entertainment, and most importantly .... CHOCOLATE!

Baby Expo
949/443-3735
Held at Phoenix Civic Plaza, this event showcases products for expectant and new parents.

March

Agricultural Day
Patriots Park in Phoenix
602/542-0998
You'd never know it to look at downtown Phoenix, but farming and ranching is a big part of Arizona's heritage and current commerce. On Ag Day, you can come see and buy and taste all sorts of stuff from the state's farming communities.

Air Show Spectacular
Williams Gateway Airport in Mesa
480/774-9355

Aloha Festival
Heritage Park in Phoenix
602/262-5071
A celebration of Hawaiian Culture, with authentic music, entertainment, crafts and food.

Mesa Day Miniature Parade and Festival
480/644-2351
Pioneer Park
Community parade and day-long family event.

Arizona Spring Fling
Central Arizona Riding Academy in Chandler
480/963-1310
dressage event

Art Detour
Downtown Phoenix
602/256-7539

Buckeye Bluegrass Festival
623/386-2727

Cactus Cup Bike Race
McDowell Mountain Park
480/926-4009

Festival of the West
Rawhide in Scottsdale
602/996-4387
A celebration of the Old West, complete with celebrities, vendors with Western gear and several arena shooting and horse events.

Heard Museum Indian Fair
602/252-8840

Irish Fest
Margaret Hance Deck Park in Phoenix
602/280-9221 or 602/404-8004

Exclusively Little
McCormick-Stillman Railroad Park in Scottsdale
480/312-2312
One-day fair for kids 6 and under.

The Paradise Valley Jazz Party
480/948-7993

Chandler Ostrich Festival
480/963-4571
The cries of "Save the Ostrich Festival" were heard, and the recent move to end the traditional

pig races/ostrich derby/eat-a-lot, see-a-lot festival have been quashed. Long live the ostrich!

Pioneer Days Parade
Buckeye
623/386-2727

Scottsdale Arts Festival
480/994-2787

Tempe Spring Festival of the Arts
downtown Mill Avenue
480/967-4877

ChicagoFest
480/833-7150
Celebration of all things Chicago, especially as it relates to the Cubs' spring training in Mesa.

Native American Artist Invitational
Fountain Hills
480/837-1654

WorldPort
American Graduate School o
Management
623/930-2963
Glendale's celebration of the nati
ethnic festival with music, danc
crafts, entertainment and childrer

Cowboys f

In

April

Asian Festival
Patriots Park
602/971-8933

Spring Fling Fest
Scottsdale Stadium
602/488-2014
Arts and crafts festival.

Cave Creek/Carefree Fiesta Days Rodeo and
Parade 480/488-3627 or 3381

...r Kids Celebrity Youth Rodeo and Family Day
602/942-5431

...ddition to the rodeo, this non-profit group's ...ain event for the year raises money for local charities with a chili cook-off, game booths, vendors and a celebrity basketball game.

EarthFest
Symphony Hall Terrace in Phoenix
602/240-2408

Numerous activities to celebrate the state's Earth Day, including Valleywide beautification projects, student contests, and environmental expo and a high-school outreach program.

Dolly Sanchez Memorial Easter Egg Hunt
Peoria Sports Complex
623/773-7137

Candy hunt, carnival games, rides, kite flying. May be held in March if Easter comes early.

Foodstock
Heritage Park in Phoenix
602/273-7842

Vegetarian food festival, with music, food, vendors and cooking demonstrations.

Arizona's Family Womens Expo
602/207-3825

A two-day event featuring celebrity speakers, business and career advice, an "idea house," arts and crafts, cooking demonstrations and legions of products related to women.

Arizona Coin Show
480/998-4001

Coin dealers come from all over the country for this show, which also includes free appraisals, an auction for rare coins and a chance to win door prizes.

Fiesta Days
Cave Creek
480/488-3381

Parade and rodeo, vendors, food booths and entertainment.

Festival Del Nino
Heritage Square in Phoenix
602/262-5029

Glendale Oasis Jazz Festival
623/930-2299

Maricopa County Fair
Arizona State Fairgrounds in Phoenix
602/252-0717

Salsa Challenge
Scottsdale Stadium
602/955-3947
Salsa-making contest to raise money for the Hemophilia Association; also features a petting zoo and children's rides.

Scottsdale Culinary Festival
480/994-ARTS(2787)

Peter Rabbit Tea Party
Heritage Park
602/261-8948
Reservations are required and space is limited for this party, hosted by characters from Peter Rabbit.

Children's Fair
Heritage Park in Phoenix
602/834-8997
Puppet theater, storytelling, hands-on activities, crafts and games for kids.

Sunday on Central
Central Avenue in Phoenix
602/261-8069
1.5-mile long street festival, with food vendors, arts and crafts, entertainment, a pet parade and a mini-Indy car race.

Peoria Pioneer Days
623/773-7137
Festival, parade, "really big yard sale," games, entertainment.

Saturday on the Square
Heritage Park
602/262-5029
Living history tours, walking tours of downtown Phoenix and old-fashioned family activities.

Cinco de Mayo
Patriots Park
602/279-4669

Cinco de Mayo Fiesta
480/644-2351
Mexican cultural celebration in Mesa, with authentic food, music and children's' activities.

Soap Box Derby
51st Street and McDowell
602/808-8059

Phoenix Youth Festival of the Arts
Hance Park Area
602/256-3493
Phoenix Neighborhoods USA

Concerts Under the Stars
Mesa Amphiteatre
480/644-2242
Come enjoy free concerts from an eclectic mix of performers.

June

Grand Canyon State Games
480/517-9700

Amateur athletes of all ages an abilities compete throughout the year in these games, which are held at various locations around the state. There is also an essay contest, art contest, rodeo and family 5K run/walk.

Juneteenth
East Lake Park in Phoenix
602/254-5081

Summer Rodeo Series
WestWorld in Scottsdale

Rodeo Connection
Rawhide in Scottsdale
480/502-5600

Watermelon Festival
Murphy Park in Glendale
623/435-0556

Evening in the Park
480/644-2351
Family fun festival in Mesa, with old-time games,
entertainment, 10-cent root beer and ice cream.

July

Fabulous Phoenix Fourth
Wesley Bolin Plaza at the Arizona State Capitol
602/261-6861

July 4 All-America Festival
Peoria Sports Complex
623/773-7137

Gold Rush Night
Eldorado Park in Scottsdale
480/312-2408

Picnic in the Park
Riverview Park in Mesa
480/644-2351
Sports-oriented family fun festival, with games and
entertainment.

Mighty Mud Mania
Chaparral Park
This event began in 1976 and features a mud
obstacle course and other fun mud stuff for kids 13
and under.

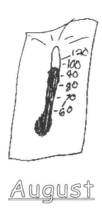

<u>August</u>

Bring in the Clowns
Rawhide in Scottsdale
480/502-5600

OASIS Gift Show
602/952-2050

<u>September</u>

Labor Day Free N Easy Weekend Celebration
Rawhide in Scottsdale
480/502-5600

Phoenix Harvest Festival
Phoenix Civic Plaza
602/262-7272

Country's largest touring arts and crafts marketplace, with more than 200 costumed artisans displaying their wares.

Hoop It Up
Arizona State Fairgrounds
972/991-1134 (FAX)
www.hoopitup.com

Entrants must be at least 8 years old. Even if you don't play, it's great fun to watch.

Alma de la Gente Fiestas Patrias
602/943-7062

Celebrates the independence of Mexico with music, food and entertainment.

Fiesta Patrias
Symphony Hall Deck
602/255-0980

Fiesta Patrias
Glendale
623/930-2960

Front Porch Festival
downtown Glendale
623/930-2960
Arts and crafts, entertainment, food.

Fiddlers Old Time State Championship
Payson
520/474-5242

So Long to Summer Fest
Gilbert
480/503-6200 or 480/898-5665
Live music, clowns, children's activities and food vendors.

Harvest Festival
Phoenix Civic Plaza
707/778-6300
www.harvestfestival.com
Hand-crafted, made-in-the-USA products; no commercial or imported objects.

Chandler Jazz and Rhythm Fest
480/786-2518

Labor Day PRCA Rodeo
Williams
520/635-4061

Renaissance Faire
Los Olivos Park in Phoenix
602/256-3130

October

Air Fair
Scottsdale Airport
480/840-9005

Rawhide Halloween
Rawhide in Scottsdale
480/502-5600
A slew of activities, including a haunted hotel,
trick-or-treating, entertainment and music and a
laser light show.

Lizard Man All-Terrain Bicycle Race
Wickenburg
520/684-5479

Columbus Day Parade
Phoenix
602/254-5521

Fiesta Bowl Duck Race
480/350-0911

Indian Rodeo
Arizona State Fairgrounds
602/252-6771

Halloween Monster Bash and Balloon Illumination
Peoria Sports Complex
623/773-7137
Interactive games, story area, carnival.

Junior League Gift Mart
602/234-3388

Mesa Pow Wow
480/644-2351
Native American gathering, featuring dance competition, arts and food.

Octoberfest
Hayden Square in Tempe
480/350-8181 or 831-1244

Pumpkin Festival
Duncan Family Farm in Goodyear
Schnepf Farm in Queen Creek
Youngs Farms in Dewey
see Farms and Dairies section for numbers.

Railfair
McCormick-Stillman Railroad Park in Scottsdale
480/312-2312
Two-day event centered around trains, with displays, face painting and educational information.

Friends of the Library annual book sale
602/534-2286

Arizona State Fair
Fairgrounds and Colosseum in Phoenix
602/252-6771

Boo! at the Zoo
The Phoenix Zoo
602/273-1341

Arizona's Family Fun Fest
Phoenix Civic Plaza
602/207-3825 or 800/880-3976
Entertainment and interactive games for families with kids of all ages, plus free food samples, sports activities, exhibitors and a mascot parade.

Chandler Cotton Festival
480/782-2995
www.arizonacottonfestival.com
Parade, racing pigs, pumpkin patch, live entertainment, petting zoo.

November

Bluegrass Festival/Annual Four Corners States Fiddlers Championship
Wickenburg
520/684-5479

Holidays Out West Fest
Scottsdale Stadium
602/488-2014
Arts and crafts festival. Patrons are urged to

contribute canned food, which will be donated to St. Mary's food bank.

Festival of Nations
Scottsdale Civic Center
480/312-2330
Celebration of different cultures from around the world, featuring entertainment, arts and crafts and food vendors.

Fiesta of Lights Street Fair
Downtown Phoenix
602/261-8604

Hispanic Fest
Peoria Sports Complex
623/773-7137

Fall Folk Festival and Quilt Show
Heritage Park in Phoenix
602/262-5071
Quilt auction and antique quilt display, walking tours, crafts for children.

Fountain Festival of the Arts
Fountain Hills
480/837-1654

Glendale Veterans Parade
Murphy Park
623/581-2500

International Christmas
Bank One Center
602/221-1005

This free display presents dozens of individual trees decorated by different ethnic groups in the area, plus dolls, carvings, a creche and other art. Choral concerts are presented regularly by local student choirs. Ethnic holiday food available. Through December.

Goodyear Cool Desert Jazz Festival
623/935-6384

Arizona Classic Jazz Festival
Mesa
480/348-3702

Veterans Day Parade
480/644-2351

Mesa's annual parade featuring bands and vets' organizations.

Veterans Day Celebration
McCormick-Stillman Railroad Park
480/585-8827

Luke Days
Luke Air Force Base in Glendale
623/856-6011

ZooLights
Phoenix Zoo
602/273-1341
Through December.

Scottsdale Desert Fall Festival of Fine Arts
480/837-5637

Fountain Hills Thanksgiving Day Parade
480/837-1654

Thunderbird Balloon Classic
Westworld in Scottsdale
602/978-7208

Fountain Hills Festival of Arts and Crafts
480/837-1654

Gilbert Days Festival, Rodeo and Parade
480/380-8399

(Check out --- or enter your own mutt in --- the dog races. It's pretty funny, although I must say that in one particular competition in the not-too-distant past, my dog was robbed. Tripped, actually).

December

Fiesta Bowl activities begin
480/350-0900

Arizona National Livestock Show
Cowboy Classics Western Art & Gear Show
Arizona State Fairgrounds
602/258-8568

Indian Market
South Mountain Park
602/495-0901

Noche de las Luminarias
Desert Botanical Garden
480/941-1225

Messiah Sing-a-Long
Scottsdale Center for the Arts
480/994-ARTS(2787)

Live Nativity
Cave Creek
480/488-3381

Canyon Lake Nautical Parade of Lights
480/671-0000

Holiday Lights
McCormick-Stillman Railroad Park
480/585-8827

Fiesta of Lights Parade
Downtown Phoenix

Cowboy Poet Christmas
Wickenburg
520/684-5479

Tempe Fall Festival of the Arts
Downtown Mill Avenue
480/967-4877

Victorian Holiday Celebration
Heritage Park in Phoenix
602/262-5071
Entertainment, children's activities, craft demonstrations and vendors.

Phoenix Feline Fanciers Cat Show
480/391-3976

Noche de las Luminarias
Desert Botanical Garden
602/941-1217

Glendale Glitters Holiday Light Extravaganza
623/930-2960

Peoria's Oldtown Holiday Festival
Osuna Park
623/773-7137
Choral contest, snow-play area, scavenger hunt, crafters, haywagon rides, children's crafts, cookie decorating and food booths.

Family Fun Zone
Heritage Park in Phoenix
602/262-5071
A New Year's Eve celebration for families, with activities and entertainment.

Afternoon Delights

Maybe it's 110 degrees out and you're looking for something to do indoors. Or perhaps you're flat broke and you just can't get excited about another trip to the park. Whatever your requirements, the Phoenix area is chock-full of ways to kill a few hours.

In this section:

Kid Stuff • Libraries
Miniature Golf and Batting Cages
Skating Rinks

Kid Stuff

Fairytale Brownies

6280 W. Erie Street in Chandler, in the South Park
Business Center
602/276-9643
www.brownies.com.

Most of the tours are for school groups, but there
are some exceptions, so call ahead. And is it worth
it? Does the term "free samples" mean anything to
you?

McCormick-Stillman Railroad Park

7301 Indian Bend (at Scottsdale Road)
480/312-2312

₂ Railroad Park

ἰ. in Chandler (McClintock
ιdler Blvd.)
)40-1685
jreat for birthday parties,
ιything where you want to
154

entertain a large group of people. They're also a nice place to go when you just have a kid or two you want to entertain. Both have cheap train rides and other rides, plus playgrounds, picnic tables and water-spraying spouts. The one in Chandler is a little tough to locate the first time you go, though; look for Desert Breeze Blvd. about a quarter-mile north of Chandler Blvd.

SuperKids Club
Superstition Springs Mall
480/832-0212

The local Fox affiliate sponsors weekly activities in the mall for young children. Storytellers, musicians and other activities comprise this program, plus participants also get discounts on activities around town.

Metrocenter Kids Club
I-17 and Peoria Avenue
602/678-0017

Held every Wednesday morning from 11 to noon near the food court, this club is for kids age 1 to 12 and provides entertainment and fun activities.

Cerreta Candy Company
5345 W. Glendale Avenue in Glendale
623/930-1000

When we went we lucked out --- or, as my husband would say, we had more luck than brains --- by showing up just as a tour was beginning. Usually, there are just two quick tours a day, and when I say quick, that's what I mean. The facility is really just one huge room where the guides tell visitors a little about some of the candy-making machines. You get lots of free samples, though, so really you can't go wrong. Just don't drive across town for Cerreta's alone; have other west-side destinations in mind, too, to round out your visit.

Webster's World of Reading
Desert Sky Mall, 75th Avenue and Thomas Road
623/245-1400

One evening each week, celebrities and community volunteers read to club members who can earn prizes based on the number of books they read.

Walkabout Arizona
P.O. Box 38605, Phoenix 85069
602/280-9951

This walking club organizes a couple dozen indoor and outdoor all over the Valley each month, plus many post-walk activities such as breakfast out. Send a SASE for more information.

chance to use their imaginations in all sorts of real-life settings.

Tyke's World Indoor Playcenter
NW corner McClintock and Southern
480/491-6017
$

This combination toy store/testing center is a great place to go if you want to keep the kids distracted while you shop for their birthday presents. They get to try out all the big playscapes while you browse the shelves or the catalog, or, my personal favorite, just sit and do nothing for a few minutes.

Enchanted Island
Encanto Park, 7th Avenue and Encanto Blvd.
602/254-1200
rides priced individually

A 10-ride amusement-park area for kids 2 to 10 years old. Rides include a carousel and ferris wheel.

Superstition Springs Center
480/832-0212

A playground inside the mall, so the kids can use up all their energy while Mom sits and eats her Dippin' Dots.

Miniature Golf and Batting Cages

Most includes arcades --- with my personal favorite, air hockey --- and snack bars.

Fiddlesticks Family Fun Parks
1155 W. Elliot Road in Tempe
480/961-0800
and 8800 E. Indian Bend Road in Scottsdale
480/951-6060

Castles & Coasters
I-17 and Dunlap Avenue
602/997-7575
Also home to Golf N' Stuff
160

CrackerJAX Family Fun Park
Greenway and Scottsdale Roads in Scottsdale
480/998-2800

Golfland-Sunsplash
155 N. Hammond in Mesa (US60 and Country Club)
480/834-8318

Scottsdale Family Golf Center
8111 E. McDonald (at Hayden)
480/991-0018

Robo Pitch Stadium
1829 E. Main Street in Mesa
480/844-0489

Batting range with baseball and fast- and slow-pitch softball machines.

Kiwanis Park Batting Range
6005 S. All-American Way in Tempe
480/350-5727

Baseball Palace Indoor Batting
1919 W. Peoria Avenue
602/997-7255

Bataway
10002 N. 12th Street (at Cave Creek Road)
602/997-7798

Rip City Batting Range
1045 E. Juniper Road Avenue in Gilbert (off Lindsay
between Guadalupe and Elliot)
480/497-9548

Steve's Strike Zone
1605 N. Hayden Road in Tempe (at McKellips)
480/990-7742

Triple Crown Enterprises
5103 W. Thomas Road in Phoenix
602/233-1007

Skating Rinks

Ice Skating

CellularOne Ice Den

9375 W. Bell in Scottsdale
480/585-RINK
www.coyotesice.com

Ice Chalet

3853 E. Thomas Road in Phoenix
602/267-0591

Ice House on McDowell

19th Avenue and McDowell

Oceanside Ice Arena

1520 N. McClintock in Tempe
480/947-2470

Polar Ice

7225 W. Harrison Street in Chandler
(1 block east of I-10)
480/598-9400
15829 N. 83rd Avenue in Peoria
623/334-1200

Roller Skating

Great Skate of Arizona
10054 N 43rd Avenue in Glendale
623/842-1181

Shadow Mountain Roller Skating Center
2616 E. Greenway Road in Phoenix
602/971-2166

Spectrum
1101 W. Ray Road in Chandler
480/917-8634

The Rink-the-Rink North
19232 N. 38th in Phoenix (North)
602/569-4459
1120 N. McClintock in Tempe (South)
480/967-0405

Skateland
7 E. Southern in Mesa
480/833-7775

Surfside Skating
1625 E. Weber Road in Tempe
480/968-9600

Rollero Family Roller Skating Center
7318 W. Indian School Road
602/846-1510

Story Times and Libraries

Story Times

Story times and book discussion groups, as well as other fun events for children and young people, are constantly going on at local bookstores. Check out newsletters from your local Barnes and Noble, Borders, Bookstar, or Changing Hands or other independent bookstore, or call direct.

Also, new in recent years are mother-daughter book clubs, which provide an amazing way for moms and their daughters to connect, and young-adult clubs based on popular series such as the American Girls. Again, ask about specific programs at your local bookstore.

Storyline
602/262-4868
602/262-4039 en Espanol

Children who come home from school alone can call in and hear a story.

Library Branches
http://pac.lib.ci.phoenix.az.us

Apache Junction Library
480/983-0204

Avondale Library
623/932-9415

Buckeye Public Library
310 N. 6th Street
623/386-2778

Chandler Public Library
222 E. Commonwealth Avenue
480/786-2312

Desert Foothills Public Library
38443 N. Schoolhouse Road in Cave Creek
480/488-2286

Gilbert Public Library
480/539-5100

Glendale Public Library
5959 W. Brown Road
623/930-3530

Mesa

Dobson Ranch Branch
2425 S. Dobson Road
480/644-3444

East Branch
635 N. Power Road
480/644-3183

Main Branch
64 E. 1st Street
480/644-3100

Phoenix

Acacia Branch Library
750 E. Townley Avenue (near Dunlap and Central)
602/262-6223

Central Library
1221 N. Central Avenue
602/262-4636

Central Branch Library
1750 E. Highland Avenue (near Camelback and 20th)
620/262-7411

Cholla Branch
10050 Metro Pkwy East (near Peoria and 31st)
602/534-3770

Desert Sage Branch Library
76th Avenue and Encanto
602/262-4636

Harmon Branch Library
411 W. Yavapai Street (near Buckeye and 7th
Avenue)
602/262-6362

Ironwood Branch Library
4333 E. Chandler Blvd.
602/534-1901

Juniper Branch Library
1825 W. Union Hills Drive
602/534-3900 (near 19th Avenue)

Mesquite Branch Library
4525 Paradise Valley Pkwy North (near 44th and
Cactus)

Ocotillo Branch Library
102 W. Southern Avenue (between Central and 7th
Avenues)
602/262-6694

Palo Verde Branch Library
4402 N. 51st Avenue (near Campbell)
602/262-6805

Saguaro Branch Library
2808 N. 46th St. (near Thomas)
602/262-6802

Yucca Branch Library
5648 N. 15th Avenue (near Camelback Road)
602/262-6787

Scottsdale
Arabian Library
10187 E. McDowell
480/391-6200

Civic Center Library
3839 Civic Center Blvd.
480/994-2474

Mustang Library
10101 N. 90th Street
480/391-6061

Palomino Branch
north Side of Desert Mountain High School
480/391-6100

Tempe Public Library
3500 S. Rural Road
480/350-5555

Tolleson Public Library
9555 W. Van Buren Street
623/936-7111

County Libraries

Aguila Branch
520/685-2214

El Mirage
14010 N El Mirage Road
623/583-1030

Fountain Hills
16836 E. Palisades Blvd.
480/837-9793

Gila Bend
202 N. Euclid Avenue
520/683-2061

Library Center
17811 N. 32nd Street
602/506-2957

Litchfield Park
101 W. Wigwam Blvd.
623/935-4118

Queen Creek
22407 S. Ellsworth Road
480/987-3600

Sun Lakes
9666 E. Riggs Road
895-5123

Surprise
15844 N. Hollyhock Street
583-0626

Laveen
9401 S. 51st Avenue
237-2904

Having a Ball

Sporting Events Across the Valley

Portland doesn't have a football team. No amount of money could buy baseball spring training for Minneapolis. Folks in Seattle don't have a major-league hockey team to call their own. And big-time college sports in San Antonio? Forget about it. But here, we have it all. Whether your family digs NCAA track and field, NASCAR or plain old NBA basketball, you're always in luck.

Several of the Valley's teams, including ASU and the Coyotes, offer family ticket packages for certain games, so don't forget to ask about special deals when you call for tickets.

Phoenix Coyotes

602/379-PUCK or 602/379-2800 for info

If you've never been to a hockey game and aren't sure if you will like it, you might want to think about going for the cheapest seats possible the first time around. Sure, you won't be able to see nearly as well as if you shell out a couple hundred bucks for seats close enough to count the blood ↑ the glass, but if your 4-year-old cries ↑he noise, or your 9-year-old complains you how bored she is, you won't feel nearly of really ↑ing.

the game, though, at some point ↑k the bank for a pair (or two) ↑elieve me, ice hockey is a lot

174

different in person than (
surprised to find yourself eag
next fight or body slam into
okay. You're in good company.

Arizona Diamondɩ

Bank One Ballpark
602/514-8400

We started taking our kids to Diamondback games
before our youngest was even 2. Of course, he is a
ball-obssessed little guy, so he loved it. The girls,
who unlike their brother have lives that extend
beyond sports, also enjoyed going, not so much for
the game itself but for the *scene.* You get to eat
nachos and hotdogs and Cracker Jacks and
strawberries and cream, and sing "Take Me Out to
the Ball Game" and be out after dark and watch
rattlesnake graphics on the big screen. Pretty cool.

If you are a planner, call early enough and you could
snag picnic-table seats, or even a spot poolside. And
the first 100 fans to the ticket gate before each
game pay just $1 for their not-behind-home-plate-
but-still-in-the-ballpark seats. That's great for
those of us who would rather spend our money on
important things. Like bratwurst.

Cox Clubhouse at Bank One Ballpark
602/462-6427
Free for ticketholders and open only on game days,

-miss part of the Diamondbacks
or kids and adult fans alike. There are
ive games, memorabilia on loan from
erstown and current and vintage uniforms and
quipment on display.

In-depth tours of the BOB are also available by
calling 602/462-6799.

Finally, the Diamondbacks **Strike Zone Kids' Club** is
for kids 15 and younger. Members pay a low fee
(about $12) and receive a T-shirt, gym bag,
newsletters and ballpark discounts. Pick up
applications at Circle K, or write to Strike Zone
Kids' Club, P.O. Box 2095, Phoenix 85001.

• • •

Fall League
602/496-6700

This is the development league for up-and-comers
and major-league players who needs work on their
basic skills. Go cheer on the Scottsdale Scorpions,
Mesa Saguaros, Grand Canyon Rafters, Peoria
Javelinas, Phoenix Desert Dogs or Sun Cities Solar
Sox in October and November.

• • •

Spring Training

The worst thing about baseball here is that throughout most of the Diamondbacks' regular season (beginning in April), it's just too dang hot. Problem solved: Go see some spring training games, played weeks and weeks before we hit the triple digits.

San Diego Padres
Peoria Sports Complex
16101 N. 83rd Avenue
623/412-7110

Anaheim Angels
Tempe Diablo Stadium
2200 W. Alameda Drive
888/99-HALOS or 602/438-9300

Chicago Cubs
Hohokam Park, Dwight Patterson Field
1235 N. Center Street in Mesa
602/964-4467

Milwaukee Brewers
Maryvale Baseball Park
3600 N. 51st Avenue in Phoenix
602/247-7177

Oakland Athletics
Phoenix Municipal Stadium
5999 E. Van Buren in Phoenix
602/392-0217

San Francisco Giants
Scottsdale Stadium
1408 E. Osborn Road in Scottsdale
602/990-7972

Seattle Mariners
Peoria Stadium
16101 N. 83rd Avenue in Peoria
602/878-4337

Dillards 602/503-5555
Ticketmaster 602/784-4444

· · ·

Arizona Cardinals
Sun Devil Stadium on Tempe's ASU campus
602/379-0101
We waited so long for an NFL football team in the
Valley, the least we can do is go see them, right?
Okay, okay, maybe you are one of the legions of
people who moved here from somewhere else and
have made a solemn vow to support the team you
grew up with until the day you die. That's fine!
Chances are, the Cardinals play them at sometime,

and you won't be the only one in the stands who isn't wearing red and white.

Regardless of what team is closest to your heart, professional football is great fun. Heck, even if you are the only one in your party who is not a football fan, you've just got to be a fan of some of the other things associated with going to a game. Again, you're going to have you nachos, for one thing, and big ol' hotdogs. Or lace up your Nikes and walk a few laps around the stadium with the kids. They'll think you're a sport.

.   .   .

Arizona Rattlers
602/379-7800
America West Arena

Arena football, as evidenced by the rabid, loyal crowd it draws, is hot, hot, hot. Faster-paced and more intimate than the traditional variety of football, arena football is riding a wave of popularity in the Valley. It incorporates the action of soccer, the structure of football and the it's-not-over-'till-it's-over feel of basketball for a whole new sports experience. The loud music they blare makes you feel like you were at a rock concert when a football game suddenly broke out.

.   .   .

Arizona Sahuaros
Peoria Sports Complex
623/516-2133

In the rest of the world, soccer is IT, the sport for which entire cities shut down and nations sent into a funk or a frenzy, depending on a single game's outcome. So why not here? Well, we've got other sports, such as football and baseball, that we have grown up with. But drive by any grassy area during the fall and spring and you will see mobs of soccer kids, soccer moms and soccer dads, proving that this sport has spread like wildfire over the past two decades. The great thing about going to see the Thunder is that you will get to see what all the fuss is about --- outstanding athletes playing a fast-paced, easy to understand game. Unlike all those folks in other countries, though, the chances of your family members getting their heads stomped by fanatical soccer hooligans is almost nil. You can't lose.

. . .

Arizona Thunder
602/263-KICK (5425)

This is soccer, too, but played indoors and on a smaller field. One difference between the two is that indoor soccer is a little more faced-paced. Outdoor soccer is "World" soccer, meaning it is what is played internationally and what you see in the World Cup and the Olympics.

. . .

Phoenix Suns
America West Arena
602/379-7800

Long before professional football and ice hockey and baseball came to the Valley there was the Suns. And even though some of the spotlight they used to own outright has to be shared now with Phoenix's other teams, the Suns are still the Suns, an exciting, always-in-the-running squad. Sure, we all wear our D-Backs gear proudly, but walk through any park or mall in Phoenix and I bet you'll still see more purple and orange than any other color combo. There's got to be a reason, right? Go to a game and see for yourself what all the fuss is about.

. . .

Phoenix Mercury
602/252-WNBA
America West Arena, 201 E. Jefferson

They said it wouldn't last. Women can't dunk. No one will watch on TV, and no one will buy tickets. There won't be any of the excitement that Michael Jordan and guys like that bring to the sport.

Basketball isn't basketball without all that testosterone radiating off the court.

Well, they were right about a couple of things. The WNBA is lacking one thing that you see plenty of in the guy's league: Infighting. Fisticuffs. Egos bigger than their shoe sizes. What you will see is a lot of talented athletes who work hard at their sport and so far have proven to be good role models for all our daughters. Our sons, too.

. . .

Phoenix Mustangs
602/340-0001
Veterans Memorial Coliseum
Following minor-league hockey is a lot like being a fan of minor-league baseball. What you give up by bypassing the majors (big names, big arenas), you make up for in other things, such as cheaper ticket prices and a feeling of intimacy with the team and the other fans. Everybody can love the Coyotes and buy their posters at the mall, but Mustangs fans belong in a more exclusive club. Another advantage: You never know when you might be watching the next Wayne Gretzky. Someday you --- or your kid --- can say that you were there before he hit the big-time.

ASU Spo

480/965-3482 for gene
480/965-2381 fc
Pac-10, Division 1A progra
basketball, football, tra
gymnastics, soccer, softball,
tennis, cross-country, volleyb

action of
races
wate

What could be cooler for a kid playing his or her first season of basketball or soccer than getting to see how the big guys --- or gals --- play? And here again, when it comes to big-time sports such as football, whether or not you or your kids are true diehard fans of the game is not necessarily as important as all the other stuff, like tailgate parties and listening to the band and seeing all the idiots with their chests painted. And doing something together as a family.

. . .

Firebird International Raceway
20000 Maricopa Road in Chandler
602/268-0200

This is the spot to go to see year-round drag-racing and special events such as "Bug-O-Rama" in April and the "Truckin' Nationals" in October. The appeal of drag racing, of course, is that you don't have to wait for them to drive 300 laps to see who the winner is. Kids love the noise, the lights and the

...this kind of event, and FIR has special
...joing on all year long on the track and in the
...r.

. . .

Manzanita Speedway
35th Avenue and Broadway
602/276-7575

Well, what you've got here is your sprint cars, your
midgets and dirt modifieds, your superstocks,
factory stocks and bombers. If, like me, you have no
idea what that means, I'll tell you what my guy at
Manzanita told me:

"The sprint cars are specially designed cars with
600-horsepower engines that run on the half-mile
or third-mile track. The Midgets are 4-cylinder,
superlightweight cars. The stock cars come in three
types ... yada yada yada ... This is grassroots racing,
a training ground for Indy drivers." Got it?

They sell earplugs, too.

. . .

Phoenix International Raceway

7602 S. 115th Avenue in Avondale

623/252-3833

A year ago if you would have told me that I would voluntarily watch car racing on television I would have told you you were crazy. But I confess that's it's addictive. In my family, we divide up all the NASCAR Hot Wheels cars that qualify for each race, then cheer our guys on.

Now, I know what you're thinking: This woman has no life. Maybe so. But if you haven't watched NASCAR in the past few years I guarantee you will be surprised at how much it has changed. In the old days, all the drivers were little guys with scraggly hair and mustaches and real bohunk accents.

Now, though, you've got a new breed of drivers who drive cool cars emblazoned with logos from businesses other than oil, tool and tire companies. What businesses, you ask? Well, M&Ms for one. And McDonald's and Corn Flakes and the Cartoon Network.

Sure, it's still a bunch of cars driving fast around a track, but once you start watching you will see that there's a lot more to it than meets the eye. Seeing it in person is even better --- a lot different from watching it on TNN. And if you're a fan of scraggly hair and hick accents, well, there's still some of the Old Guard around.

All for One and One for All

Into every life a little rain must fall, right? Well, when it does, there are people here to help. And even in the good times, we could all use a little support, which is why there are so many parenting groups and classes available across the Valley.

In this section:

Resources • Moms Clubs and Parenting Groups   Parenting Classes • Giving Back Hot Links • Play It Safe

Resources

Community Information and Referral
602/263-8856 or 1-800 352-3792

Clearinghouse for various services across the Valley for those in need.

Entrepreneurial Mothers Association
602/788-3083

Arizona Families for Home Education
602/443-0612

East Valley Family Resource Center
480/834-9424

Single Parents Association
602/788-5511

Phone Friend
480/829-0599, extension 105
Run by the Association for Supportive Child Care,
this program allows for latchkey kids to call and
check in with an adult after school.

Child Care Resources and Referral
602/244-2678
Free child-care referral service with huge database
of daycare centers and in-home caregivers.

Childhelp USA
1-800-422-4453
Child-abuse hotline.

Childrens Resource Center
602/483-9130

Family Matters
480/755-0479

Jewish Family and Childrens Services
623/486-8202

Mentally Ill Kids in Distress
602/253-1240

Offers assistance in raising behaviorally challenging kids.

Nuestra Familia
623/936-3980

A family-support agency offering help with life skills and provides counseling in the west Valley.

Project SPINE @ the Glendale Youth Center
623/934-0419

Non-profit program for drug prevention and the promotion of social responsibility.

Pregnancy and Breastfeeding Hotline
602/258-2900

Governor's Division for Children
602/542-3191

Advises the governor on issues related to children. Call for info on conferences

Companion Animal Association of Arizona
602/995-5885
This group has a great Pet Grief Support Service for anyone going through the illness or death of a pet.

Multiple Joys
602/756-1239
Support for families of twins, triplets and beyond...

Parents Anonymous
1-800-352-0528 or 602/248-0428
This group offers assistance to anyone who needs support in relating to their kids calmly. This is whom to call if you ever feel out of control and in danger of crossing the line between positive discipline and child abuse.

Child Abuse Hotline
1-888-SOS-CHILD (767-2445)
Whom to call if you suspect someone of abuse or neglect of a child.

Special Needs

Pilot Parent Partnerships/Special Kids
602/242-4366

Support system for families of children with disabilities or special needs, with legal information and on-site lending library.

Arizona Early Intervention Program
602/941-2199

A clearinghouse for information and referrals for families needing assistance in special-needs areas.

Southwest Human Development
602/266-5976

A human-services organization that administers health and education programs for children up to age 6 and their families.

Children's Information Center
602/256-7577

A clearinghouse serving special-needs children and their families.

LaLeche League of Phoenix
602/234-1956
Information and support on breastfeeding, plus support groups around the Valley.

Moms Clubs and Parenting Groups

Parenting Development Institute @ Gateway Community College Parenting Groups
602/392-5185
The PDI's parenting classes usually develop into moms clubs all over the Valley. Call for information on what's available in your area.

Family Resources "Steps"
480/834-9424
East Valley parenting groups for babies and toddlers.
First Steps Together, for newborn to 8 months old, Stepping Together (8 months to 3 years), and Playgroup, for ages 2 to 5.

Moms on the Move
602/675-INFO(4636)

Support group for new moms, with two branches in the northeast Valley.

MOMversations
480/460-4959
www.momversations.com

A sort of parenting group in monthly newsletter form. It is "for all moms, "focusing on what we all have in common rather than on our differences," says its founder and editor. Education, health and safety, humor and support are the backbone of this publication.

Ahwatukee Mothers & Friends
CeCe Mack, 480/961-8688

A safe haven for at-home moms in the Ahwatukee area, with group activities for moms and kids such as playgroups, babysitting co-ops and social activities.

Central Phoenix Homeschool Support Group
Lydia 602/266-9961

Desert Ridge Parenting Group (Northeast Phoenix)
Mary Beth 480/502-4411

North Central Parenting Group
Nancy 480/502-3860

Entrepreneurial Mothers Association
602/892-0722

A support and information group for mothers who own their own businesses.

Homemakers by Choice
602/241-6360

Nondenominational Christian women's Bible study group that meets weekly in northeast Phoenix.

MOPS (Mothers of Preschoolers)
1-800-929-1287
Call for local branch information.

McDowell Mountain Ranch Parenting Group
480/563-8844

MOMS (Moms Offering Moms Support) Clubs

These non-profit clubs for stay-at-home moms usually have monthly meetings, plus mothers' night out, children's field trips and playgroups, and special-interest groups such as scrapbook groups and book clubs.

There are now more than 40 MOMS Club chapters across the state; for information on a chapter in your area, call the East Valley area coordinator at 480/857-6262, the West Valley area coordinator at 623/561-5898, or the state coordinator at 480/837-0671, or send $2 for a brochure to MOMS, 25371 Rye Canyon, Valencia CA 91355. You can also send an e-mail to momsclub@aol.com with "local chapter info" in the subject line, or visit the organization's web site at www.momsclub.org.

Foothills Women's Club
480/460-0699

Arizona Mothers of Multiples
602/840-0869

Mothers of Multiples 507-0380 for Gilbert, Chandler or Mesa, or 473-0882 or 788-1519 for PV, Fountain Hills and Scottsdale.

Mothers of Twins Club
623/561-9374
7 chapters Valleywide

Northwest Phoenix Moms Club
Robin 602/582-4938

Insight for Moms
480/894-2201, extension 241

Bible study and social club for mothers of all denominations; meets at Grace Community Church in Tempe.

The National Association of Mothers' Centers
www.motherscenter.org
Christine 480/596-0148
or Patricia 602/942-0718

A Mothers' Center is where mothers can share experiences, learn about parenting, and make friends. The center provides lectures, support/discussion groups and social activities. The focus is on the woman, not necessarily on the children or on parenthood. The local branch meets in Scottsdale.

Parenting Classes

Most hospitals and many churches also offer parenting classes, as well as those on CPR, breastfeeding, birthing and sibling adjustment.

East Valley Family Resource Center
480/834-9424
Agency to provide support through parenting classes, classes for children and classes on familial relationships.
Information Line: 480/834-9365.

Glendale Family Development Center
623/934-7001

Parenting Development Institute @ Gateway Community College
602/392-5185
Various classes and workshops offered all over the Valley regarding child development, family interaction and stress management.

Parenting Skills Program
480/967-6895
Tempe-based program offering a variety of classes.

PEP Promoting Educational Partnerships
480/730-1087
Seminars and referrals regarding educational issues.

Southwest Human Development
602/266-5976
Classes on discipline, communication and self-esteem.

Parent University
480/472-0377
Mesa Unified School District-run classes designed for adults who want to help their children reach their full potential.

Academic Advocacy and Consultation
602/270-1987
Offers service for a fee designed to help parents obtain the best possible education for their child.

Babies R Us
480/705-0400
Various parenting classes.

The American Red Cross
602/461-1100
Classes in CPR and first aid, of course, plus more on having a healthy pregnancy and a healthy, safe family.

Children's Resource Center
480/483-9130
Parenting workshops.

Family Matters
Classes from early pregnancy on. 480/755-0479.

Giving Back

Volunteer opportunities abound in the Phoenix area, including those that would be perfect for families to do together. You can build new trails, feed and walk animals at your local shelter or deliver meals to elderly shut-ins. If you desire to give of your time, rest assured that there is a perfect fit for you, regardless of your interests and schedule.

Volunteer Center of Maricopa County
Central Office: 602/263-9736
East Valley Branch: 480/461-3198
The Center puts out a book each year listing Phoenix-area volunteer opportunities, with each

entry detailing the type of work and preferred age level for volunteers.

National Family Volunteer Day

Usually in November, this is a day in which parents and their kids can participate in various projects to help their communities. Call 1-800-865-8683 for more information on what's going on in the Valley.

Get Those Knees Up

Another great way to give back to others is to participate in walks for charity. Nearly every Saturday from September through May there are 10Ks, fun runs and walks to raise money for various charities. For a minimum donation (usually $10 to $25), you can get a T-shirt, get some exercise, spend some quality time with your family and help out a good cause. And don't be afraid if the name of the event is "Half Marathon" or "10K;" virtually every race event has divisions for walkers.

If you have a favorite charity or cause, chances are it will be represented by a road race/fun run sometime during the year. Smaller races, though, are sometimes one-time events or jump around the calendar from year to year. You will have to check with the sources listed below to keep up with those kinds of events. Also, while nearly every race benefits a cause, the recipient charity can change from year to year.

Check out the websites www.raceplaceevents.com or www.arizonaroadracers.com to get information about, and even register for, upcoming races, or call 602/277-4333. Below is a listing of the ones you can usually count on occurring in the Valley:

January
Runners Den 10K

February
Lady Footlocker 5K
Sunrise Kiwanis Mountain to Fountain 15K

March
Mayo Clinic 8K run
United Healthcare 5K

April
Run of the Mill 8K

May
Rural Metro Night Run for the Arts

June, July and August
Are you kidding? It's too hot to walk anywhere!

September
Schlotsky's Evening Bun Run

October
Race for the Cure (Breast Cancer)
Maricopa County/United Way 5K
The Rep/Downtown YMCA Half Marathon
Fiesta Bowl Classic
AIDS Walk Arizona

November
Phoenix New Times 10K
Mesa Parks and Rec Turkey Trot

December
Midnight Madness Run

Hot Links

When I was pregnant the third time around I devoured the birth-story websites. I would read the stories of four-hour painless labors and think "See, it is possible!" And then I would read the tales of 52 agonizing hours of labor that ultimately resulted in cone-headed 13-pound babies and I would think "See, mine can't possibly be that bad!" Either way, I was reassured.

For new moms, the Internet offers up a whole world beyond ratty, spit-up-stained bathrobes and leaky breasts. For those with evolving families, there are safety tips and advice on everything from bed-wetting to paying for college.

Included here are some of the most stable, helpful family and parenting sites on the Web. Whether you are trying to conceive or are about to welcome your first grandchild, there's something here for you.

For what's going on locally, try the following sites:

www.accessarizona.com has up-to-the-minute info on sports and other events, plus weather and community info.

www.phoenix360.com is another great site for newcomers as well as for those looking for local information.

For information on individual Valley cities, type in **www.ci.city.az.us**, substituting the name of the city you want to check out for the word "city." For example, www.ci.mesa.az.us will take you to Mesa's home page.

www.azfamily.com, home of KTVK-TV independent Channel 3, and WB61, offers up a wealth of information on what's happening in the Valley.

www.kaet.asu.edu features information on programming for our local PBS Channel 8.

www.kphotv5.com, CBS affiliate Channel 5's online home.

www.phoenix360.com, the site for KNVX-TV ABC 15.

www.fox.com provides information on FOX Channel 10 programming.

www.azcentral.com is the online version of The Arizona Republic. This is one of the best online newspaper sites in the country, going beyond simply reprinting its news pages. It also provides a lot of information on Valley communities, including historical bios, school and industry information and what's happening.

www.queenfortheday.com I didn't know where else in the book to included this, but I just had to put it somewhere because it is such a great idea. Queen for the Day is the brainchild of Nancy McKay, a local radio personality on AM1100. In addition to party and even planning, McKay provides the Queen service, in which the lucky recipient can design her own special day (or have it designed for her by whomever is footing the bill), choosing from luxuries such as her own personal lady-in-waiting, chauffeur service, beauty treatments and paparazzi. Check out the website or call 1-888-8BQUEEN (1-888-827-8336)

Sites for Mom and Dad

Baby Bag Online
www.babybag.com
Humor, chat, and shopping information related to pregnancy and parenting young children.

Childbirth.Org
www.childbirth.org
It's just like the name implies --- everything you need to know about pregnancy and childbirth. Includes huge amount of labor tales.

Family.Com
www.family.com
Huge Disney-affiliated site covering everything from making your own baby food to handling bullies.

The Family Web
www.familyweb.com
Participants in this site come from around the world and get together on message boards and chat rooms to discuss pregnancy and parenting issues.

Moms Online
www.momsonline.com
Excellent, well-designed site with departments such as I'm Pregnant, Mom to Mom, Ages & Stages, Home Space, Job Wise and As a Family.

ParenthoodWeb
www.parenthoodweb.com
Extensive site covering every topic imaginable.

ParentsPlace.com
www.parentsplace.com
If your kid wets the bed or your stepdaughter is plotting against you, this is the place to turn for support from others going through the same thing. Frequent expert online discussion groups, pregnancy clubs and playgroups, and what is perhaps the Web's most voluminous list of message boards make up this very useful site.

Parent Soup
www.parentsoup.com
Yet another really great site that covers trying to get pregnant to dealing with your teenager and everything in between.

Parent Time
www.parenttime.com
By the publishers of Parenting and Baby Talk magazines, this site bills itself as "the resource for kids age 0 to 6."

Positive Parenting
www.positiveparenting.com
This site takes a no-frills approach to its design but offers up some good stuff related to education and the building of happy, thriving families.

The Baby Net
www.thebabynet.com
More stuff than you can shake a stick at. The Baby Net is a clearinghouse for all things baby-related. You can get information on baby-product companies, baby catalogs, baby safety --- really, anything you need or think you might need someday.

The Mommy Times
www.mommytimes.com
This site combines a lot of interesting articles
with a half-dozen humor columns. The focus is
primarily on moms of the under-8 crowd.

Stork Site
www.storksite.com
"The premier pregnancy and new parenting
community," this spot on the Web has a very
personal, chatty feel.

The Whole 9 Months
homearts.com/depts/health/00ninec2.htm
From the fine folks who bring you Redbook, Good
Housekeeping and Cosmo, this site is all about ---
guess what? --- pregnancy.

The Family Education Network
www.familyeducation.com
In my humble opinion, this is the most useful, best
designed and interesting education-related site on
the Web. There's advice on all the things you know
you need to know (how to evaluate your child's
school), as well as advice on all the things you didn't
even know you needed advice about (the proper way
to write an excuse note).

The Daily Parent
www.dailyparent.com
Pregnancy, health, education and relationships are
covered by dozens of topics discussed by experts
and on chat boards.

The WholeFamily Center
www.wholefamily.com
A really way-cool site on marriage and parenting
that centers around the "real-life dramas" in which
real-life problems are worked out in stages. You
have to see it to get the full effect.

The La Leche League
www.lalecheleague.org
Sore? Cracked? Bleeding? Love nursing and want to
do it until 18 months but your inlaws think that's
icky? Check out the premier authority on
breastfeeding for advice and support.

PEP: Parents, Educators & Publishers
www.microweb.com/pepsite
Provides information on children and technology, and
features software reviews.

Ask A Great Granny
www.mbnet.mb.ca/crm/granny/136.html
This Canadian mother of six and grandmother of 15
uses her own experience and her degree in
psychology to answer reader questions.

Mr. Rogers Page
www.pbs.org/rogers/
This page has some great ideas for parents to
enhance their children's learning and experiences.
Also, check out the rest of **www.pbs.org** for other
educational and entertaining info.

The CyberMom Dot Com
www.cybermom.com
My personal favorite woman/mommy site on the web.
Visiting this site is the computer version of
reading Redbook on the couch, with a wide variety of
topics laid out in a visually appealing, easy-to-use
way.

Home Based Working Moms
www.hbwm.com
A web page offering support, information, and
resources to moms who are or would like to be
working
from their homes.

WAHM Online Magazine for Work at Home Moms
www.wahm.com
Ditto.

Home-Income Parents
www.hipparents.org
Advice for moms or dads who work from home our
would like to.

ChildSecure
www.childsecure.com
A site with health information, consumer recalls
and up-to-date info on the latest, safest baby
products available.

The Parenting Toolbox
www.parenting toolbox.com
This site says it offers "nontraditional tools for
nontraditional parents."

The Family Connection
www.thefamily.com
Easy-to-use site with pages on marriage, parenting,
crafts, scrapbooking, genealogy and recipes.

SalukiSearch.com
www.salukisearch.com
A family-friendly search engine you don't have to be afraid to let your kids use. A huge data base provides relevant information on nearly all inquiries.

Parent Partners
www.parentpartners.com
An education- and development-based site for parents of children up to age 5.

Families Plus Parenting Q & A
www.parenting-qa.com
Your questions are answered by those in the know.

Family Resource Online
familyresource.com
A site focusing on finances, health, marriage, lifestyles and parenting.

Kids Doctor
www.kidsdoctor.com
Articles and advice organized by an actual real-life doctor.

Parent News
www.parentnews.com
Unique site covering a wide variety of topics
related to lifestyle and family issues.

The National Parenting Center
www.tnpc.com
Home base for The National Parenting Center, an
organization dedicated to helping parents build
their parenting skills.

Let's Get it Together
www.organizedtimes.com
Offering in home organizing and time-management
skills for busy parents. Like Heloise, but more
extensive.

The Kidz Are People Too Page
www.geocities.com/Heartland/8148/
Christian-based guide to "gentle parenting."

Amazing Moms
www.amazingmoms.com
A good site for parents, teachers and Scout
leaders, Amazing Moms offers up ideas for birthday
parties, art activities and games.

Mother's Day Out
www.mothersdayout.com
Another well-rounded "mommy site" whose goal is to
"help women be at their best as a woman and a
mother."

A Mom's Love
www.amomslove.com
A little New-Agey, but still addresses all the
basics.

Stay-At-Home-Mom.com
www.stay-at-home-mom.com
A reading-based site for parents that features an
on-line book club with regular meetings, chat with
the authors and related articles.

NetWorking Moms
www.WorkingMoms.com
An award-winning web site designed to help working
mothers achieve balance between office and home.

Miserly Moms
www.miserlymoms.com
This site features tips on how moms can be wise
with their money so that they can afford to stay
home with their kids.

Mothers At Home
www.mah.org
Mothers at Home is the country's oldest and largest organization supporting stay-at-home mothers.

F.E.M.A.L.E
www.FEMALEhome.org
Home base for Formerly Employed Mothers at the Leading Edge, a support and ideas group for formerly employed moms who now stay at home to raise their children.

Manic Moms
www.manicmoms.com
Humor-based newsletter for frazzled parents.

Moms Hall of Fame
www.momshalloffame.com
For a fee, this site will display a photo of your favorite mom with a message from you.

Midlife Mommies
www.midlifemommies.com
As its name implies, this site caters to the interests of women in their late thirties and beyond.

Kid Source
www.kidsource.com
Education, health and safety-related topics.

Surfing the Net with Kids
www.surfnetkids.com

Kids Campaigns
www.kidscampaigns.org
Information for parents who want to improve their communities.

Sites for Kids

Yuckiest Site on the Internet
www.yucky.com
The Liberty Science Center sponsors this page, which teaches science concepts to kids in a way they will find fun.

World Kids Network
www.worldkids.com
A site for and by kids, at which they can showcase their talents and communicate with others from all over the world.

White House for Kids
www.whitehouse.gov/WH/kids
When typing in this address, DO NOT forget the
".gov," or you will find yourself and your kids at a
porn site instead of the home base for our nation's
political center.

The Kids.Com
www.thekids.com
Stories, games and links covering the entire planet.

The Case
www.thecase.com/kids
Mysteries for kids to solve.

Sports Illustrated for Kids
www.sikids.com
Sports-related stories written for kids age 8-15.

National Wildlife Federation
www.nwf.org/kids
Another great learning-without-knowing-it site.

NPR Science Friday Kids Connection
www.npr.org/programs/sfkids

National Geographic Kids
www.nationalgeographic.com/kids

Kids Voting USA
www.kidsvotingusa.org
Site run by a grassroots organization dedicated to preserving democracy by involving kids in the voting process.

Smithsonian Magazine: Kids' Castle
www.kidscastle.si.edu
For ages 8 to 16, this site features sports, history, the arts, travel and science articles and activities.

Kids' Space
www.kids-space.org
Dedicated to fostering literacy, artistic expression and cross-cultural understanding.

Welcome to Kidspub
www.kidspub.org
Kids can read stories from other kids around the world, or submit their own.

Cool Science for Curious Kids
www.hhmi.org/cool science
Just what the name implies. A great way to spark your child's curiosity in science.

Funorama
www.funorama.com
An online bookstore for kids, in association with Amazon.com. You can download coloring pages or utilize other activities for kids through junior high.

Club Z
www.clubz.com
"Activities designed to stimulate young minds" in a fun, magazine-style format.

Stone Soup
www.stonesoup.com
The online version of the popular by-the-kids, for-the-kids art and literature magazine.

Homework Central
www.nosweat.com
Study site with large, comprehensive database to help with research.

Play It Safe

Pool laws, carseat and seatbelt laws, advice on water, scorpion and critter info, bike helmet info, numbers for safety coalitions

Car Smarts,
Bike Smarts
Safe Kids Coalition 602/947-4701
www.safekids.org

Under Arizona law, all children under age 5 must be in a "child passenger restraint system," otherwise known as a carseat or booster. Tethers that hold the upper part of the seat in place are not mandatory, but they do provide an extra measure of safety by making the seat more secure.

Once your child moves on from this to a seatbelt, make sure he or she sits up straight and wears the seatbelt in its proper position, across the hips. Hundreds of kids receive internal injuries every year because their seatbelts were worn wrong.

As for bike helmets, it's been proven that more than 80 percent of head injuries could have been prevented if the rider had worn a helmet. Get the kids started early so that helmets are a habit, and make sure that you wear one yourself.

Water Smarts

Pool barrier laws vary from town to town; call the number listed below for your area's specifics. Even if your city does not require a pool fence, think about getting one anyway. You always hear that it took "just a few seconds" for a child to drown or become permanently disabled. Don't wait for your own tragedy or close call to find out how true that is.

Apache Junction 480/982-4440
Avondale 623/932-6088
Buckeye 623/386-7830
Carefree 480/488-1471
Cave Creek 480/488-1400
Chandler 480/782-2063
El Mirage 623/972-8116
Fountain Hills 480/837-2003

Gilbert 480/503-6300
Glendale 623/930-2800
Goodyear 623/932-3494
Guadalupe 480/730-3080
Litchfield Park 623/935-1066
Maricopa County 602/506-3301
Mesa 480/644-2061
Paradise Valley 480/948-7411
Peoria 623/773-7225
Phoenix 602/262-7884
Queen Creek 480/987-0496
Scottsdale 480/312-2500
Sun Cities 623/974-2321
Surprise 623/583-1089
Tempe 480/350-8341
Tolleson 623/936-8500
Youngtown 623/933-8286

To prevent a drowning, keep tables, chairs or other things that can be used for climbing away from pool fences. Keep flotation devices handy, and have a phone near the pool area. And never ever ever ever leave a child alone in the pool, even for just a few seconds.

Remember, too, that children do drown in 5-gallon buckets, toilets and bathtubs with just a little water.

If you do find a child in the water, follow these steps:

• Yell for help and get the child out of the pool

• Call 911

• Begin CPR if trained. If you aren't, follow instructions from the fire department until they arrive

To learn CPR, contact your local fire department, the Red Cross, the American Heart Association or a hospital or YMCA near you.

Arizona Poison and Drug Information Center
602/253-3334
(For poisonings, bites and stings)

Critter Smarts
We share the desert with a lot of creatures who love the heat and the dry air. Here are some of the more dangerous of those and some advice from the Samaritan Regional Poison Center on what you can do if you are bitten or stung:

Rattlesnakes:
Of the 11 species of rattlesnakes identified in Arizona, the most common are the western diamondback, Mohave, sidewinder, black-tailed, speckled and tiger. The snakes are most active in

late July or August after the start of monsoon season, or anytime the weather is at least 80 degrees (usually March through October). Baby rattlesnakes, born in the summer, are just as dangerous as their larger counterparts.

Of course, the best thing you can do is stay out of the snakes' way. They are most typically found in desert areas around the edge of town. So stay alert when you are hiking; stay on the trail and keep your eyes open. Each year more than 80 rattlesnake bites are reported to the SRPC.

Signs of a bite:
• Immediate pain or a burning sensation at the site of the bite; fang marks are usually visible

• A metallic or rubbery taste in the mouth

• Significant swelling within minutes, followed by weakness, sweating and/or chills, nausea and vomiting

Treatment: Get to the Emergency Room ASAP. Don't panic, but get moving as quickly as you can.

Other don'ts:
• Don't apply ice or immerse the bite in a bucket of ice

• Don't restrict blood flow with a tourniquet or constricting band

• Don't cut the bite or try to suck out the venom

• Don't try to capture the snake to bring to the hospital

Scorpions:

There are 36 species of scorpions in Arizona, all of which can sting. Only one type of sting --- that of the bark scorpion --- requires medical treatment. Now for the bad news: that's the most common scorpion in populated areas.

The bark scorpion is small --- just one to two inches in length --- and it is light tan to dark golden brown. It is a nighttime feeder and usually found near irrigated areas, pools, in palm trees and wooden fences and on the walls in homes. It can climb and walk across ceilings, and sometimes winds up falling into bathtubs, sinks and beds. Yeeeesh! It is most active when the temperature is at least 70 degrees.

Okay, now I'm going to tell you a story that will keep you awake for many nights to come. When I lived on a ranch in high school we had a scorpion problem. One night my mother woke up in the middle of the night. Having been stung before, she knew immediately by the pain ("like holding a lit cigarette to your skin," she says) that she had been stung. So, she got up and turned on the lights. She looked under the covers and around the bed and couldn't find the guy who'd stung her. The she felt something and turned her head .... AND THERE ON HER SHOULDER WAS THE SCORPION. AND HE WAS SMILING! Well, okay, he wasn't smiling. But it still freaked her out, as did the EIGHT OTHER SCORPIONS she found crawling around when she pulled the bed away from the wall. Apparently their point of entry was a small hole in the baseboard behind her bed. Pretty awful, huh? Anyway, back to business ...

Children are most susceptible to developing severe symptoms from scorpion bites, so if you live in an area where they are prevalent, you may want to put netting across your baby's crib and place the crib legs inside wide-mouth jars. Also, pull back the sheets and check for scorpions before you get into bed, and wear shoes when you are outdoors. Nearly 5,000 stings are reported annually in the Valley.

Signs of a sting:
• In infants and children there will be immediate crying, rapid, jittery eye movements and increased salivation

• Pain, of course. No swelling or redness. Intense pain to the touch

• Numbness and tingling moving to parts of the body distant from the sting. Infants and children may rub the face, indicating numbness there

• Uncoordinated eye movements

• Difficulty swallowing and excessive drooling. "Swollen tongue" sensation

• slurred speech

• Restlessness and irritability

• Possible respiratory problems

Treatment: Call the poison control number above to determine whether the sting can be managed at home or will require treatment.

Black Widow

These spiders are most often found down low, under outdoor furniture or grills, wood piles or the corners of porches and patios. They are most active at night.

The tough part is that to kill these suckers, you've got to directly hit the adult spider with a strong insecticide and destroy the egg sacks. So, you've got to wait until it's dark, get a flashlight and go a'huntin'.

Signs of a bite:
• The initial bite might feel like a pinprick, or go unnoticed altogether. A red circular mark may appear about six hours after the bite.

• The victim may feel progressively more achy, with muscle pain at the site spreading to the lower back, arms and legs. Symptoms can last up to 36 hours and lingering effects can last several weeks.

Treatment:
Call the SRPC. Most of the 350 bites in the Valley each year can be managed at home.

Conenose Bug

Here's another really sick predator --- one I had never heard of before. This guy, called the "kissing bug," is dark brown to black with yellow and red markings. It is about an inch long, with three pairs of legs and a cone-shaped head. It spends nights in birds nests, but during the day it may come inside and hide under furniture or in closets.

Here's the sick part: The kissing bug is so named because it bites and feeds on the blood of its victim when the victim is asleep. The good news is that there aren't many of these types of bites reported locally. However, once you are bitten you are more likely to develop more severe symptoms (itching scalp, palms and soles; a rash; nausea) if you ever get bitten again. Call the SRPC if you suspect you been, uh, kissed.

Gila Monster

You've got to be pretty unlucky to get bitten by a gila monster, as they spend less than two weeks each year above ground. They are like the ultimate snowbirds.

If you do get bitten, though, you'll know it. That's because once the gila monster bites, the gila monster does not let go. You will have to pull it off. Do so quickly, as the longer he stays attached, the more venomous his bite.

Symptoms of a bite:
• Pain, and a lot of it
• Swelling, weakness, dizziness and chills

Treatment:
• Get the thing to let go of you and get to the hospital right away

There are other biting, stinging things around, such as ants, wasps and yellowjackets, plus coral snakes and fiddleback spiders. No fiddleback bites have been reported in the Valley. If you are bitten by anything and have symptoms that are severe or may signal an allergic reaction, call 911 or the SRPC.

Other things you can do to prevent bites and stings in your home:
• Remove debris from your yard; don't have a big woodpile

• Wear gloves when working outside

• Keep doors and window tight-fitting, and fix all cracks in the foundation

• Look before you put your hand under something

• Examine all line-dried clothing before bringing it into the house

• Don't leave shoes or towels outside

Yucky Stuff Smarts

The following plants, shrubs and trees are poisonous: caladium, crown of thorns, dieffenbachia, flowering bulbs (amaryllis, crocus, daffodil, hyacinth, paperwhite), lily of the valley, pothos, philodendron, schefflera, azalea, calla lily, castor bean, Carolina jasmine, century plant, chinaberry tree, English ivy, fox glove, iris, lantana, larkspur, Mexican bird of paradise, morning glory, oleander, rhododendron, star jasmine, sweet pea, Texas mountain laurel, wisteria, plus apple tree seats and peach and apricot tree kernels and some wild plants and trees.

First Aid for ingestion of these and other dangers in the home (from cleaning supplies, medicine or antifreeze):
• Remove any remaining substance from the mouth

• Call the SRPC before doing anything else. It will be helpful if you know what was swallowed and how much, as well as the weight of the child.

If something gets in your child's eye, flush the eye with lukewarm water poured from a glass two to three inches from the eye, or take him into the shower. Repeat for 15 minutes. Do not force open the eye.

What is NOT poisonous: asparagus fern, African violet, Boston fern, coleus, dandelion, dracaena, impatiens, jade plant, marigold, orchids, peperomia, petunia, poinsettia, prayer plant, purple passion vine, rose, rubber plant, snake plant, spider plant, Swedish ivy, wandering Jew, wax plant, yucca, zebra plant, zinnia.

Weather Smarts

When I first moved here no one told me about the monsoons. I was pumping gas one August afternoon about four days after my arrival when the sky turned green, the wind picked up and sand and dust flew through the air. Within minutes a storm was raging.

We are lucky here in that we don't have tornadoes or hurricanes or earthquakes. What we do have is really, really, dangerously hot weather for a few months every year, and the monsoons. The heat can cause heat exhaustion and heat stroke, or more commonly for children and young people, simple dehydration.

The monsoons bring flash floods, lightening and high winds. If you can avoid going out during these storms, do. And whatever you do, if you see a flooded low-water crossing, don't try to cross it. It's just not worth it.

And last but not least, if you're going to be outdoors
Don't Forget The Water!

Next up from Michelle Burgess:

10 States in 10 Weeks
How my family rediscovered the West and each other without going broke or insane

Due in time for Christmas 2001
(If I survive the trip, that is)

I could use your help with this one. Our planned route takes us from Arizona through the following cities and areas: Albuquerque, Santa Fe, Colorado Springs, Denver, Vail, Salt Lake City, Jackson and Yellowstone National Park, Bozeman, Helena, Idaho Falls, Twin Falls, Boise, western Oregon, Seattle, Portland, Eugene, the coastal highway in California, Santa Rosa, San Francisco, Sacramento, Lake Tahoe, Carson City, Yosemite National Park, Las Vegas and the Grand Canyon National Park. We aim to hit nine state capitals (everywhere but Wyoming). If you have visited these spots and know of great hotels or must-see attractions, e-mail me at hottogo@uswest.net or write to Michelle Burgess, 1520 W. Warner Road, Suite 105, PMB #110, Gilbert 85233 and give me your suggestions. A free copy of "10 States" will be awarded to the first person to submit an idea that is included in the book.

Thanks for your help. Wish me luck!

A Parents' Guide to Life in the Valley of the Sun

Michelle Burgess

To order additional copies of
"Phoenix for Families"
Please send $14.95 per book
(plus $4 Shipping and Handling for the first book
and $1 each additional book) to:

Hot To Go Publishing
1520 West Warner Road • Suite #105 • PMB #110
Gilbert, AZ 85233

_____ Yes, Please send me _____ copies of
"Phoenix For Families"

@ $14.95_____ + S&H _____ = _____

Please send to:

Name _____

Address _____

City _____ State_____ Zip_____

Phone _____

E-Mail Address _____

237

Notes

Notes

Notes